REPORT ON THE SHROUD OF TURIN

Report on the
Shroud of Turin

John H. Heller

Boston

HOUGHTON MIFFLIN COMPANY

1983

Library of Congress Cataloging in Publication Data

Heller, John H. (John Herbert), date
Report on the Shroud of Turin.

Bibliography: p.
1. Holy Shroud.   I. Title.
BT587.S4H44   1983   232.9′66   83-127
ISBN 0-395-33967-7

Printed in the United States of America

V 10 9 8 7 6 5 4 3 2 1

For Maria, my wife, and Wallace A. C. Williams

Remember, we have yet to figure out how to deduce Hamlet from the molecular structure of the mutton chop.

—*Thomas Huxley*

Acknowledgments

This book is a report on the research performed on the Shroud of Turin by a team of forty scientists. It is the story of the investigations carried out by these men and women, as seen through my eyes as a team member. It does not include the individual stories of the entire team, for if it did it would have been the length of *War and Peace*. Hence, more is omitted than is included. Though I am the "least of the brethren," my role is not proportionate, for the activities that were most vivid to me were those in which I participated. The members of the team were scattered across the land and abroad, and an enormous amount of work took place in individual laboratories where only the investigators directly involved were privy to the day-to-day work. The rest of us shared our data at frantic weekend meetings hither and yon across the country.

To obtain the details of those events at which I was not present, I traveled extensively and taped interviews with team members who exercised endless patience as the hours droned on. Due to scheduling conflicts, a few were missed. To all who were obliging with their time, my thanks and appreciation.

I am particularly indebted to A. Adler, E. Brooks, R. Bucklin, T. D'Muhala, D. Devan, R. Dichtl, R. Dinegar, J.

viii

Druzik, W. Ercoline, J. Gambescia, J. German Jr., R. Gilbert, M. Gilbert, J. Jackson, E. Jumper, R. London, D. Lynn, G. Markoski, V. Miller, R. Morris, R. Mottern, S. Pellicori, G. Riggi, R. Rogers, L. Schwalbe, and B. Schwortz.

I am indebted to His Majesty King Umberto II of the House of Savoy and to Archbishop-Cardinal Anastasio Balestrero of Turin for their time and courtesy.

Special thanks are rendered to Professor Luigi Gonella of the Politecnico di Torino, whose expertise aided and supported the team's research in Turin and my efforts with this book.

Colleagues from the East to the West were generously obliging in providing input. The following helped with specific questions: J. Gall, G. Hutchinson, W. Kahn, G. McCorkle, J. Pelikan, A. Shestack, and B. Skinner, Yale University; E. Adkins and D. Seligson, Yale University School of Medicine; S. Freedberg, Harvard University/Fogg Art Museum; B. Benacerraf, Harvard Medical School; C. Vess and G. Vikan, Harvard/Dumbarton Oaks; E. Clark and W. Zoller, University of Maryland; P. Damon, University of Arizona; R. Prinn and I. Newell, Massachusetts Institute of Technology; R. Stoiber, Dartmouth College; A. Norris, University of Texas; G. Wasserberg, California Institute of Technology; C. Welbourn, Ohio State University; F. Filas, Loyola University (Chicago); A. Cameron, University of London; H. Lamb, University of East Anglia; H. Sadoff, Michigan State University; G. Carter, East Michigan State University; W. Rose, Michigan Technological University; M. Saltzman, University of California at Los Angeles; A. Mills, University of Leicester; W. Bulst, Techniche Hochschule Darmstad; A. Whanger, Duke University.

In addition, the following were most helpful: D. Shepherd, Cleveland Museum of Art; G. Russell and J. Rosewater, Smithsonian Institution; N. Kajitani, The Metropolitan Museum of Art; T. Husband, The Cloisters; J. Plummer, J. Pierpont Morgan Library; H. Kasimir, National Oceanographic and Atmospheric Administration; R. Hunter, U.S.

Geological Survey; R. Frosch and M. McCormick, National Aeronautic and Space Administration; R. Cadle, National Center for Atmospheric Research; G. Ruggieri, New York Aquarium; B. Cameron, Children's Hospital Medical Center Research Foundation, Cincinnati; H.Lee, Connecticut State Crime Laboratory; B. Dixon, Center of Forensic Sciences, R.C.M.P.; M. Siliato, Rome; G. Abbott, Melbourne, Fla.; and K. Weaver, National Geographic Society.

Frs. Adam Otterbein and Peter Rinaldi put up with all types of outrageous nonsense from me and earned the deep gratitude of the team, for without their intercession we never would have been able to test the Shroud.

Wallace A. C. Williams, friend and mentor, provided the yeast without which this work would not exist. Other helpful members of the clergy included M. Weaver, A. Dreisbach, V. Donovan, C. Stubbs, and T. Bourne.

Traveling back and forth across the United States, Italy, England, and Portugal to conduct interviews and additional research for the book could not have been completed without the aid of a travel grant from the Pope Foundation, with particular thanks to Catherine, Fortune, and Anthony Pope.

I am fortunate to have two friends, Allan Sloane and Hillary Waugh, both authors, whose encouragement and critical comments were most important.

My wife, Maria, with her incredible attic whose contents the team shared, is a most special person. Throughout the four years of research and writing she could and did call a spade "a bloody shovel" when she felt it was needed. She endured my self-frustration with stoicism and added psychic jet fuel when I foundered.

To the children of the house, Sandra, Julien, Susan, Yvette, Kathleen, Christopher, and Adrian, who dissented, clucked, nodded, argued, and provided significant input, I tender my paternal gratitude and love.

For help through problems large and small, which arise in the writing and publishing of a book, my appreciation to Austin Olney, an editor with a gentle and compassionate touch. Jeffrey Seroy of Houghton Mifflin spent much time and effort culling the manuscript. Lois Rindner provided able editing and, along with Margaret Palmer, typed circa 3000 pages of tape transcripts and manuscript. To them my thanks. Copy editors come in various colors — usually from gray to black. Mine, Frances Apt, was stellar, with all the warm luminosity of a rainbow. She was a joy to work with.

Finally, thanks to the late John L. Senior, Jr., whose interest, financial support and concern will remain enduring.

There were many others who must go unacknowledged due to limitations of space and the immense size of the undertaking.

Contents

Prologue

THE SHROUD OF TURIN is a linen cloth, fourteen feet long and three and a half feet wide. The threads were hand-spun and the fabric hand-woven in a three-to-one herringbone twill.

On the long fabric are two faint, straw-colored images, one of the front and the other of the back of a nude man who was apparently scourged and crucified, with the hands crossed over the pelvis. The images appear head to head, as though a body had been laid on its back at one end of the fabric, which was then drawn over to cover the front of the body.

The cloth has many burn holes and scorches; the holes have been patched. There are also large water stains. Although the cloth appeared in France 630 years ago, its history is obscure.

The Physics of Miracles?

By faith, I am a Christian; specifically, a Southern Baptist.

By profession, I am a scientist; specifically, a biophysicist.

By genesis, I am a New Englander, with all the skepticism and conservatism of the breed.

All this being the case, I have always felt that relics are nothing but flummery from the Dark Ages.

In 1978, I had never heard of the Shroud of Turin, let alone seen a picture of it. When I did, I was surprised. I thought I would see something analogous to all the paintings and statuary of Jesus that I had ever seen. I had viewed Oriental portrayals of Christ in Japan and China, and black ones in Africa, a host of medieval and Renaissance forms in Florence and elsewhere in Europe, as well as Byzantine and modern versions.

This was different. It was anything but artistic. In addition, everything was reversed. Its images were like photographic negatives, with black and white, left and right, reversed. The cloth was also very bloody, with the "nail holes" in the wrong place; they were in the wrists, not in the palms. There were large scorch marks and burn holes down both sides of the fabric. The man was nude, his hands folded over the groin. I did not know at the time that the photograph I was looking at had been enhanced; the actual images were so faint that they could not be seen from up close, but only at a distance of about one or two yards. Yet if one was too far away, they faded into the background of the cloth. I could not imagine a more unlikely object for veneration.

Then I was shown photographic negatives of the Shroud, which made the human images become positive. This helped considerably by showing a man in a way familiar to our perception. However, now the blood was negative, or white, which detracted from the whole. To say I was still unimpressed would be an understatement.

About a month later I read a report by Dr. Robert Bucklin, the deputy coroner and forensic pathologist of Los Angeles County. Dr. Joseph Gambescia, a pathologist in Pennsylvania, concurred in the findings.

Forensic pathologists specialize in causes of violent death, and it was this report which first caused my eyebrows to rise a bit. I have, tucked far away in my background, an M.D., though I do not use it much. I had also spent eight years on the faculty of Yale University School of Medicine: two in pathology and six in internal medicine. The forensic report said (with some translation from the medical jargon):

> Irrespective of how the images were made, there is adequate information here to state that they are anatomically correct. There is no problem in diagnosing what happened to this individual. The pathology and physiology are unquestionable and represent medical knowledge unknown 150 years ago.

That, I thought, is a remarkable statement.

This is a 5-foot, 11-inch male Caucasian weighing about 178 pounds. The lesions are as follows: beginning at the head, there are blood flows from numerous puncture wounds on the top and back of the scalp and forehead. The man has been beaten about the face, there is a swelling over one cheek, and he undoubtedly has a black eye. His nose tip is abraded, as would occur from a fall, and it appears that the nasal cartilage may have separated from the bone. There is a wound in the left wrist, the right one being covered by the left hand. This is the typical lesion of a crucifixion. The classical artistic and legendary portrayal of a crucifixion with nails through the palms of the hands is spurious: the structures in the hand are too fragile to hold the live weight of a man, particularly of this size. Had a man been crucified with nails in the palms, they would have torn through the bones, muscles, and ligaments, and the victim would have fallen off the cross.

I had never known or thought of that, but, of course, that is just what would happen.

There is a stream of blood down both arms. Here and there, there are blood drips at an angle from the main blood flow in response to gravity. These angles represent the only ones that can occur from the only two positions which can be taken by a body during crucifixion.

That made physiological sense to me.

On the back and on the front there are lesions which appear to be scourge marks. Historians have indicated that Romans used a whip called a *flagrum*. This whip had two or three thongs, and at their ends there were pieces of metal or bone which look like small dumbbells. These were designed to gouge out flesh. The thongs and metal end-pieces from a Roman flagrum fit precisely into the anterior and posterior scourge lesions on the body. The victim was whipped from both sides by two men, one of whom was taller than the other, as demonstrated by the angle of the thongs.

There is a swelling of both shoulders, with abrasions indicating that something heavy and rough had been carried across the man's shoulders within hours of death. On the right flank, a long, narrow blade of some type entered in an upward direction, pierced the diaphragm, penetrated into the thoracic cavity through the lung into the heart. This was a post-mortem event, because separate components of red blood cells and clear serum drained from the lesion. Later, after the corpse was laid out horizontally and face up on the cloth, blood dribbled out of the side wound and puddled along the small of the back. There is no evidence of either leg being fractured. There is an abrasion of one knee, commensurate with a fall (as is the abraded nose tip); and, finally, a spike had been driven through both feet, and blood had leaked from both wounds onto the cloth. The evidence of a scourged man who was crucified and died from the cardiopulmonary failure typical of crucifixion is clear-cut.

The description read like a modern coroner's report of a violent death. It reified the event. I suddenly realized that it cleared up a point that had always bothered me. I know the thorns of the Middle East, and I didn't see how anyone who wasn't wearing metal gauntlets could twist those thorns into the twined circlet-type "crown" that is shown in most depictions of the Crucifixion. I had been a classical civilization major at Yale and could still recall bits and pieces of ancient history, so I knew that the Romans did not use metal hand armor. But the lesions on the man could have been made by the kind of crown that covers the whole head like a cap. Using a sword and some twine, I could make one of those from several boughs of thorn without destroying my hands. I also recalled that Roman citizens were protected from whipping by the flagrum, because it was considered too cruel.

The parallels between Bucklin's report and the Gospel accounts were obvious. The departures from convention — the size of the man, the form of the crown, anterior scourging, two men, flagrum, wrist holes, all the accurate pathological physiology — gave the Shroud an aura of verisimilitude.

I looked at the photos again. This time they appeared slightly less alien.

Could, I wondered, these images on the cloth have been caused by some products of body chemistry? I began to think rapidly through all kinds of chemical reactions that might be possibilities, however remote. After about ten minutes, I could think of nothing that made any sense at all. This was a stem-winder, all right. It had to be a forgery.

But if it was, whoever had painted the images must have been a person of considerable genius.

This forensic evaluation was actually my second exposure to the Shroud. The first had been from impeccable scientific sources. At the time, I would never have deigned to consider such a subject had it been under any less prestigious intellectual auspices.

I regularly read my weekly copy of *Science,* the world's most widely read scientific journal. It covers all areas of science, and new discoveries are often announced between its covers. One spring evening, as I recall, I was perusing it while lying on a couch in postprandial contentment, when I shot upright.

"Good grief," I barked, *"the physics of miracles?"*

My wife, Maria, who is normally immune to my expostulations, asked, "What is that supposed to mean?"

"This article is a report on a group of scientists who are investigating the Shroud of Turin."

"Why," queried Maria, "should that surprise you?"

Though Maria is a Catholic, I seldom have been circumspect about my views. I answered, "You know how I feel about relics. I'll bet if you took all the pieces of the True Cross and put them in one place, you'd have a lumberyard."

The *Science* article had been written by Barbara Culliton, one of the finest science reporters in the country. Although most of the researchers involved in the project were unknown to me, they all came from first-rate institutions. These included the California Institute of Technology's Jet Propulsion Laboratory (JPL), best known to the public for its magnificent photographs of the planets, the Los Alamos Scientific Laboratory, which is generally associated with nuclear bombs, the U.S. Air Force Academy, Sandia Laboratory, and others. Such places attain their excellent status only from the scientific stature of the men on their staffs.

The group's leader was Dr. John Jackson of the Air Force

Academy. Two names — Walter McCrone and Ray Rogers — were familiar to me. McCrone was an analytical chemist who specialized in identifying particles by microscopy; he ran a commercial laboratory in Chicago. Rogers was an explosives chemist on the staff at Los Alamos.

The article stated that McCrone was independent of John Jackson's team. He had become well known in 1974, when Yale University asked him to examine a map it had acquired, which it and other experts judged was made around 1440 in the Rhineland. On this map, there was an outline of a land mass in the New World that was labeled "Vinland." Such a map, predating Columbus by fifty years, was obviously a rare and important cartographic event. McCrone claimed that the ink on the map was made from a material that had been synthesized only since 1920, and he stated that the likelihood of the Vinland map being authentic was analogous to "that of Admiral Nelson's battleship at Trafalgar being a Hovercraft." The debunking was front-page news across the nation. The Yale library was abashed.

Because of his work in explosives, Ray Rogers was an eminent expert in thermal effects. His initial interest in the Shroud was fanned by the observation that it had been through a fire in 1532, at which time parts of the silver box containing the cloth had melted. Molten metal had burned through the layers of folded material, intersecting areas of "blood" and body image, and leaving ugly holes and scorched areas down both sides of the linen.

Rogers realized that this mischance had created a first-rate thermal experiment. *Science* reported Rogers' thoughts. He knew the melting point of silver made during the Middle Ages. Silver was virtually never pure; it always had contaminants, such as mercury, copper, lead, and arsenic, any or all of which would place the melting point at about 900°C. He calculated that the temperature within the box had risen to nearly 200°C, before the box was doused with water. This permitted him to calculate roughly the temperature gradient across the linen and to make certain deductions about the images. He realized that if the blood and body had been created by an artist using any organic pigment — or even an inorganic pigment in an organic vehicle — the heat would have produced a significant change in color in portions of the images. This would also be true if the images were made in whole or in part of such biologic materials as aloes and myrrh. However, the photographs of the Shroud, both in black and white and in color, showed no effect whatsoever.

Rogers had written, "If large, complicated, natural products, or organic products were responsible for the image, they should have decomposed, changed color, or volatized at different rates, depending on their distance from the high-temperature zone during the fire. There is no evidence for any variation at all."

This made excellent scientific sense. Nonetheless, it seemed to me that the likelihood of the Shroud being a forgery was still overwhelming. Both sense and science, as well as prejudice, went into this judgment — perhaps in equal parts.

I turned to consider that portion of the article which discussed something I could not comprehend at all. It mentioned that the images on the Shroud seemed to have three-dimensional attributes. It went further and said that the investigating scientists had produced a three-dimensional re-creation of the man in the Shroud.

I deemed this to be patently impossible. A true 3-D image created from a 2-D photograph is physical nonsense. After all, a photograph has only height and width. The third geometrical dimension, depth, is provided by the brain of the viewer.

To make the problem even more strange, an ordinary photograph of the Shroud is a two-dimensional image of another two-dimensional surface — the linen cloth itself, which is also flat. There seemed no obvious way that a 2-D picture of a 2-D surface could be manipulated by mathematics or an electronic device to give a 3-D image. It was just too ridiculous.

On the other hand, the scientists mentioned in the article in *Science* were from the image-enhancement team at the Jet Propulsion Laboratory. They had been involved in the Viking space probe, and their pictures from space and from Mars were absolutely outstanding. If these men claimed there was 3-D information that could be transmitted from one flat surface to another, to an analytical machine that processed it, the investigators must be seeing something. Just what, I could not fathom.

Whereas I tended to discount the 3-D comments, I did pay attention to another claim by the JPL team. While processing the photographic image and feeding data into an IBM 370/65 computer, a massive brute, they looked at various characteristics of its intrinsic structure. They found that it had a "wide range of spatial frequencies," which were oriented in a random fashion. This meant that no matter how the images on the linen had been formed, it was not likely that they had been made by a human hand. If they had been painted, brush marks would have been picked up by this technique. Furthermore, no method of applying anything by hand can be directionless. But if the structure of the images was random and truly directionless, that would indicate strong presumptive evidence that no human hand was involved. This observation was intriguing as well as disquieting.

The conclusion *Science* came to was that the Shroud was (1) the product of an extraordinarily ingenious forger, (2) a rare but explicable phenomenon, or (3) the result of the physics of miracles.

No matter which of the three was right, this had to be an incredibly challenging project.

But, I thought, so what? So are astrophysics, genetic engineering, immunology, anthropology, and subatomic physics, in many of which disciplines I'm involved. Why get stirred up by a Catholic relic?

The article ended by saying that Jackson's team would probably be permitted to examine the Shroud in several months, and a confrontation between science and religion would occur, with no outcome guaranteed.

I decided to dismiss the whole subject.

The following morning, as I was shaving, the phrase "the physics of miracles" popped into my head.

It's just a clever phrase, I thought. That Shroud *has* to be a forgery. Things like that were made in the Middle Ages — and before and after.

I went off to my office at the New England Institute and proceeded to submerge myself in work. I have been an academic for the past thirty-five years, having held only two jobs, the first at Yale and the other on the faculty of the institute. The institute's fundamental research is at the intersecting areas of physics, chemistry, and biology. Its investigators are all cross-trained in several fields and usually work on the cutting edge of the unknown.

During the course of the morning, I received a call from an old friend and colleague at MIT. After technical matters were out of the way, he asked whether I had read the current issue of *Science*.

"Yes," I replied, standing up at my desk. "Why?"

"Did you see that Culliton article on the Shroud?"

"Yes. Why?"

"What did you think?"

"Well, it's pretty far-out, but it certainly sounds challenging."

"Oh, brother! You're going to get involved."

Puzzled, I asked, "What put that silly idea into your head? I plan to file it and forget it. What a curious thing for you to say!"

"No, it isn't, and you won't."

"I won't *what?*"

"Forget it. I've known you for years, and you never use the word 'challenging' for a project without getting involved up to your neck."

Startled, I said, "Really? I never knew that. I don't believe it. Are you sure?"

"Dead sure. It's never failed. But this one's bound to be controversial, so mind your butt."

Bemused and confused, I hung up. Was I really so predictable? Did I really give other people signals that predicted my behavior but of which I was unaware? The whole thing was unsettling. The more I thought about it, the more annoyed I became. "I will not get involved," I growled, "if for no other reason than to cross up that smartass at MIT."

When lunchtime came, I took *Science* out of my briefcase to read the article once more, just to prove to myself that I would not, and could not, get involved in this peculiar archeological artifact. As I read, my negative frame of mind began to melt and give way to puzzlement. I noticed one sentence I had missed the previous evening: "Given the hubris of contemporary science, it is not surprising that Shroud researchers are confident that, given time enough, they can explain how the image of the man in the Shroud came to be."

That bothered me, because I felt the same way. I had always believed that hubris was the second greatest sin of a scientist — the greatest being falsity. This made me very uncomfortable. I recalled reading in college that pride was the worst of the seven deadly sins. That struck me at the time, and I surprised myself by remembering it all these years. "Hubris" is the Greek word for overweening pride.

This Shroud is not like the mythic Holy Grail, I mused. It is a real, palpable thing. Science is damn good at measuring things! That is our specialty. This cloth is made up of atoms and molecules, which we can identify. Hubris or no, it is absolutely impossible that science will not come up with the answers. I still had much to learn.

By this time my afternoon was in shambles. I was obviously flirting with the idea of becoming involved. To resolve some of my conflicting thoughts, I resorted to an old trick taught me by my father. Taking a large pad, I drew a line down the middle and labeled one column "Pro" and the other "Con." Deciding that the Con column was the easier one, I began with it:

1. It is undoubtedly a forgery — 95% probability.
2. If not, it is some kind of curious natural phenomenon — 4.999999% possibility.
3. The physics of miracles? A 0.0000001% possibility — and fading fast.
4. There is already a team. If they wanted someone like you, they would have one on board by now.
5. What makes you think they would accept if you volunteered?
6. If you got involved, you would be smack in the middle of a controversial subject. No matter what happens, some group will be furious. And that group may be made of donors to your scientific research or members of a grant committee, and who needs that?
7. There are many in the academic community who will unquestionably regard this as (a) a boondoggle, (b) something fit only for religious nuts, (c) unsound, etc.
8. *Science* mentioned some involvement by a Holy Shroud Guild, which sounds like a Catholic enterprise. This may be a project to legitimize a relic, in which case you absolutely do not want any part of it.
9. If you became involved, it would take time away from research, teaching, fund-raising, administration, as well as your family, and you cannot afford it.
10. You are up to your armpits in fascinating scientific problems now. You do not need another one.

Then I turned to the Pro column. Hard as I tried, I could only find one item:

1. It sounds challenging — maybe incredibly so.

It was clear that the cards were stacked massively against my participation. I put the lists in my pocket and went home early — and took *Science* with me.

The following morning when I arrived at my office and opened my briefcase, I realized that I was still lugging around the Culliton article. I sat thinking for about five minutes. I pulled out my Pro and Con lists and finally said aloud, "It *is* challenging. It might just be the most intriguing thing I have ever heard. It can't hurt to test the water. I can always back out."

Suiting action to thought, I called in my secretary and dictated a letter to Professor Jackson. Scientists can always contact one another, whether or not they're acquainted. A quick look at a standard reference — *American Men and Women of Science* — gives the complete background and bona fides of each of us.

I wrote to Jackson: "I have just read the article in *Science* on the Turin Shroud. Several things puzzle me. I cannot, for the life of me, understand the reference to a 3-D image. Surely, one cannot 'create' a 3-D image from a 2-D surface. If I have misunderstood, I would appreciate your insight. The man is represented by an image. The other subject is the blood. Is it an 'image' of blood, or is it actual blood? If it is the latter, it should be very simple to determine."

Jackson wrote back: "Thank you for your letter. In reply to your question on the image, I am enclosing a Xerox of an article from the 1977 conference on the Shroud. As far as the blood is concerned, it may be actual blood, but no one seems to know. It was tested in 1973, but unsuccessfully."

The enclosed Xerographic copy of the 3-D image was so poor that I could make nothing of it, so I let that sit for a moment. However, I did reply about the blood. In part, I said: "I do not understand what an 'unsuccessful' blood test is. It is either positive or negative. There is nothing in between."

Rather than replying through the mail, Jackson called. He told me that in 1973 some Italian scientists had taken out a "blood"-covered thread, tested it, and could not obtain a positive result. But, they added, it was not negative. He wanted to know what I meant by my comments on the blood tests. I replied that, as far as I was concerned, what he had just reported was double-talk. If one had a bloody thread, one would have to be extraordinarily inept not to be able to measure it.

Jackson wanted to know why. I told him that members of the institute staff had been working with blood porphyrins and had learned how to make them fluoresce; hence, we could obtain a light signal and . . .

After a while, I realized that I was carrying on a monologue, and stopped.

Jackson said, "Well, I'm basically a physicist, and I don't think I've been following you. Besides, in 1973 there were two forensic scientists on the team that examined the Shroud, and they couldn't find blood. But they said a negative test didn't mean anything; only a positive one would have."

"That's nonsense. Either it's there or it isn't. What exactly did they do?"

"I don't know precisely, but, then, I'm a physicist. If you like, you can look at Ian Wilson's book on the Shroud. He discusses it there. It's just out, so you should be able to find it anywhere."

"Right. I'll get it and call you back."

I hung up and, figuring my afternoon was probably shot anyway, went to my car and drove to my favorite book emporium, which nine times out of ten had what I wanted. It had the Wilson book. I returned home and read it straight through. The book was quite entertaining, but Wilson's science was awful. I knew from my own studies that his history was a fanciful collage, and I suspected that his art history might be, too. Wilson was clearly sold on the fact that the Shroud was authentic, and his bias showed heavily.

The next morning, I called Jackson and told him I had read the book. "The two Italian forensic people did simpleminded tests," I said. "It's no wonder they didn't get any answers."

"Are you sure?" asked Jackson.

"Dead sure. If you don't do the right tests in the right

way, you can never get old blood into solution. If it's not in solution, you can't obtain a positive test."

"But," replied Jackson, "they're both university professors, and . . ."

"I don't care if they were the pope and the president of Italy. I read what they did and what they saw on the fiber. If that gunk on it is blood, they should have gotten so positive a test, you could see it across the room. If they didn't solubilize it, they didn't have a prayer. Of course, they could have made physical measurements and gotten an answer."

"Physics?" queried Jackson.

"Sure. Microspectrophotometry." There was a long pause.

Finally Jackson said, "Well, do me a favor. We have a first-class chemist in the group, Ray Rogers. Would you give him a call at Los Alamos and tell him what you just told me?"

"Right. I'll be back to you."

I called Ray Rogers and told him the substance of my conversation with Jackson.

"We can," I elaborated, "manipulate the porphyrin molecule and make it fluoresce." (Porphyrins are among the key molecules in nature. They are organic molecules of basically similar structure, usually with one metal atom in the center. In blood, the porphyrin has an iron atom; in chlorophyll, it has a magnesium atom. If we treat the porphyrin in hemoglobin in a certain chemical manner, we can excise the iron atom from the structure, which then can be made to fluoresce. Fluorescence is a physical process whereby a specific wavelength of light excites the molecule, which then gives off light at another specific wavelength. This emitted light can be enormously amplified and measured.)

Rogers immediately responded, "You're absolutely right. I agree with you. Porphyrin fluorescence is an interesting approach."

I called Jackson back and told him of my talk with Rogers.

"That's great. Say, you're in Connecticut, and the Shroud

team is going to meet in Amston, Connecticut, over the Labor Day weekend. How would you like to come and discuss it some more?"

I agreed. When I hung up, I reminded myself again of
the Pro and Con lists and began to worry about the cons.

Two weeks later, I received a call from Dr. Christopher
Cook in New York. He told me that he lived reasonably
close by, was a member of the Shroud team, and would like
to visit me. Incidentally, he asked, had I seen the film *The
Silent Witness?*

I said no, and asked about it. Cook told me it was a docudrama, based on Wilson's book, that portrayed some of
the team's scientists and their work.

I said I'd like to see it very much, and a date was arranged.

Cook arrived with a videotape, which he hooked to a TV
set, and we both sat back to watch. It was my first opportunity to match some faces with names in the *Science* article.
There was Dr. Robert Bucklin, deputy coroner of Los Angeles. He was in hospital greens, in a morgue, and had a
full life-size picture of the man in the Shroud — front and
back — on the wall. Very deliberately, with the typical re-
serve and understatement of a forensic pathologist, he re-
cited the diagnoses I had already read.

Then Professor John Jackson, a tall, lean, handsome young
man, with a low voice, discussed the photographic image.
His words and phrasing at once proclaimed him to be what
he had said he was, a theoretical physicist. He was followed by Professor Eric Jumper, an engineer, who described his analysis of the information contained in the photo
of the Shroud. Jackson and Jumper discussed the fact that
mathematical analysis of the Shroud images contained three-
dimensional information. They stated the obvious: a photograph has only height and width, and contains no three-
dimensional information at all.

Hearing this, I felt better about what I was seeing, which
made good scientific sense. Then Jackson placed a photo of

the man in the Shroud in a VP-8 image analyzer, *and a three-dimensional image of a man leaped out on the screen.* The newness of the technology that produced this image, and the disturbing quality of the image itself, piqued my curiosity still more. I had not even really tested the water, and already the magnitude of the challenge had increased by a quantum jump.

Now I could return to my regular activities and wait for the meeting at Amston to see whether I would choose to become further involved. I thought I had best read up on the subject of the Shroud.

I went to Yale's Sterling Library, looked up the Shroud, and was taken aback by the huge amount of literature on it. Whenever I discover a subject about which so much has been written, I feel I really *should* be familiar with it. No matter how often I recognize this combination of conceit and ignorance in myself, each time I collide with something that is well documented and of which I am completely unaware, my intellectual self-assurance feels threatened. Hubris.

So there I was, looking at index cards for dozens and dozens of references. Then I began looking at some of the bibliographies. By the time I was through, I found that there were about 275 books and other references published before 1950. They were in Latin, French, Italian, Spanish, and German, as well as in English. I was relieved that there were no references in Syriac, Armenian, Arabic, Persian, and Greek — or so I thought then.

There is always the problem of whether one should begin at the beginning of an old historical event and work forward, or whether one should start with the most recent literature and work backward. I opted for the latter course. It soon became obvious that there was a pro-authenticity group, and an anti faction. Almost no one was neutral.

I thrashed through a lot of material, much of it terribly turgid and filled with ecclesiastical bombast. It was clear that, in these attacks, authors and ecclesiastics had developed a lot of high blood pressure on this one subject. One cleric would say of another's opinion: "It is written in barbarous Latin; it is violent and incoherent in tone, abounding in obvious exaggerations, blemished by bad logic and bad theology, reckless in imputing the gravest crimes against truth, justice, and religion . . ."

After sorting through volumes of this type of rhetoric, I decided to take some shortcuts. I determined that both the pro and anti schools focused on a letter written by a bishop six hundred years ago. Why so much spleen and passion has been vented over the centuries would normally be of as much interest to me as a belch in the midst of a tornado, but, human nature being what it is, I suspected that the whole brouhaha might be resurrected again in the course of the Shroud research — almost as though it were a new discovery. I thought I had better look into it.

Naturally, I wanted to know what the bishop said, but that posed a problem. As so often happens in this type of historical controversy, book after book quoted excerpts or, even worse, excerpts of other excerpts of someone else's translation. To find out what was really said, one must go back to the original. And often the original is not easy to come by. I persevered and finally found the bishop's letter in Latin. The style of writing and invective it displayed had, I thought, been invented by *Pravda* and *Isvestia*. This bishop was not just angry — he was furious, violent, and enraged. He was paranoid, and I use that word in the psychiatric sense. Savonarola and Torquemada could have taken lessons from this bishop's prose. What had elicited this eruption of towering passion? The Shroud and its origin.

To understand this controversy, we need to know a bit of history. There was a French knight of outstanding bravery, Geoffrey de Charny. In a manner known to none, Geoffrey acquired the Shroud sometime before 1356. If he told anyone how he came by it, the story has not yet come to light. There are allusions to Geoffrey's acquisition of the Shroud by a pope, by his widow, and by his granddaughter, but the versions differ greatly. Some have suggested strongly that he received it as stolen property, and therefore would not reveal the source. Whatever the truth, Geoffrey, by-passing the local bishop, received a papal bull that established a church, under his sponsorship, at Lirey in France.

Shortly after, two battles of the Hundred Years' War intruded on the Shroud story. Ten years before, in 1346, Edward III of England, with his sixteen-year-old son, the Black Prince, defeated an overwhelmingly superior number of French knights at the battle of Crécy. Three months after the dedication of the Lirey church, the Black Prince was back in France, leading a small band of archers and knights in a *chevauchée* across the countryside. The French king, John II (Jean le Bon) was eager to wreak revenge on the English for Crécy. He called out the flower of French knighthood, among whom was Geoffrey de Charny. Geoffrey's valor was so great that King John appointed him as his standard bearer; he carried the oriflamme. King John commanded more than ten times the number of men led by the Black Prince. But once again the superiority of the British longbowmen triumphed over the heavily armored knights. King John, with but a few men, including Geoffrey, made a last stand at Poitiers. Where a lance threatened the king, Geoffrey de Charny interposed his body, to die at his monarch's feet. King John was captured and taken to England, and the secret of de Charny's acquisition of the Shroud perished.

With the king's capture, France was thrown into chaos. Geoffrey's widow fell on difficult times, and eventually permitted the Shroud to be exhibited in the church her husband had founded.

It was again being shown — three bishops and about thirty-five years later — when our choleric bishop wrote his blistering letter to the pope of the Western schism, Clement VII, at Avignon.

To summarize the missive: the cleric claimed that the Shroud was a painted forgery, and that the local church was becoming rich through the contributions made by pilgrims who came to see the Shroud. Specifically, he alleged that the bishop who had held the see shortly after Poitiers had alleged that the Shroud was an alleged forgery by an alleged painter, who allegedly confessed to having painted it. No evidence of this alleged prior series of events exists.

The pope who received the original of the letter — which has never been located — sentenced the bishop to perpetual silence on the subject. He did not preclude the Shroud from being exhibited, but told the canons of the church to say it was a "representation."

In fact, it does not make any difference what any bishop or pope did or said or did not do or say. None of them saw the Shroud. And even if they had stared at it night and day for a year, they would have been none the wiser. It makes no difference if one or ten painters or a whole atelier had claimed that they had created the Shroud. That which would be discovered by scientific methodology, beginning with the photographs taken in 1898 and culminating in the current scientific exploration, would provide answers so totally beyond the ability or competence of medieval clerics — no matter on which side of the question they stood — as to make any such argumentation ultimately trivial. Now I was about to embark on a voyage of discovery.

2

The VP-8, an Image
in Three Dimensions

DR. JOHN JACKSON had first seen a photograph of the Shroud when he was fourteen. Later, in graduate school, he found two books on the subject, and thought it might be a good topic for his master's thesis in physics. When he told his faculty adviser what he had chosen as a thesis problem, the adviser was honestly bewildered.

Fortunately, the issue did not have to be resolved, because Jackson found that, as a U.S. Air Force lieutenant, he could obtain his Ph.D. in physics at the U.S. Navy Postgraduate School in Monterey, with all expenses paid. Since he was married and had two small children, Jackson jumped at the chance.

Four years later, with his new doctorate in physics in hand, he reported to his first Air Force assignment at the Weapons Laboratory in Albuquerque. There he became involved with extremely sophisticated systems, such as laser-beam and particle-beam weapons. During his spare time he and another officer, Rudy Dichtl, a physicist and a genius at electronics, developed a hobby of hot-air ballooning. They obtained their balloon pilot licenses and wrote a how-to book that has become a standard for novices.

One day when Jackson and his brother-in-law were ballooning, the weather suddenly changed, and the winds shot up to more than thirty miles per hour. Realizing that he had better land as rapidly as he could, Jackson started an emergency descent, and the two men prepared for a crash landing. The gondola hit the ground at a severe tilt and a speed of thirty knots. The impact tossed his companion out and caused the propane tank to go to full throttle, where it acted like a giant flame thrower, kindling the dry grass and Jackson's clothing, while the whole rig hurtled and bumped over the ground. Jackson reached through the fiery chaos, slammed off the propane valve, pulled the rip cord, thus collapsing the balloon, and proceeded to put out the fires on and around him.

This side of Jackson — the man of action assessing a situation at high speed and jumping in to recover control — is not generally seen. Normally, he is a thoughtful theoretician, and his tall, lanky frame ambles along while his head seems in the clouds as he puzzles through some arcane problems in physics and mathematics. He is a young, absent-minded professor in the classic sense, and an optimist with the hallmark of a fine scientist — an unquenchable lust to know.

After the fiery landing, he decided that he would put aside ballooning for a while and undertake as a hobby his old interest, the Shroud of Turin. Now, most people would look at a photograph of the Shroud and, according to their faith and training, dismiss it or consider it an interesting, if somewhat peculiar, man-made artifact. Some might accept it as the burial shroud of Jesus of Nazareth, even though, as I was to discover later, the Catholic Church has never proclaimed it as such. It was only when the first photograph was taken, in 1898, that renewed interest in this ancient, stained, and burned piece of cloth was awakened. The photographic negative let the world see, for the first time, a positive picture of the man in the Shroud. As a result, two Frenchmen, a biologist named Delage and a surgeon named Barbet, wrote on the subject early in this century. Both worked from photographs. Delage was an agnostic, and Barbet a faithful Catholic, but both reached the same conclusion: the Shroud was authentic. However, these were opinions only and could by no stretch of the imagination be called anything more. Others held contrary opinions, and some of these, as we have already seen, went back to the fourteenth century.

What in the world would make a theoretical physicist like John Jackson undertake an investigation of the Shroud as a hobby? The same thing that drives all good scientists — curiosity, which sparks interest. Interest may be a mild word in common usage, but it is what motivated Galileo, Kepler, Newton, Einstein, and, indeed, all scientists of all times to probe the unknown. There is another mild word — fun. When researchers say something is a "fun" project, they mean, in lay parlance, that it is exciting, fascinating, intriguing, tremendous, exhilarating, and all other similar terms rolled into one. Jackson, and the men and women who accompanied him to Turin in 1978, thought that the Shroud was a fun project.

In order to tackle any new problem, a scientist begins with a hypothesis. It can range from the mundane to the outrageous, but any hypothesis is acceptable provided that it can be tested. It must be, in scientific parlance, falsifiable. Jackson began with a hypothesis that was about ten stages beyond outrageous. He hypothesized that the Shroud was, indeed, a long sheet on one end of which a corpse had been placed on its back, with the remaining cloth folded over the man's head, covering him frontally down to and beyond his toes. Then, in some manner (as yet unhypothesized), the image of the back and front of the wounded and crucified man was transferred to the linen.

A lesser man (myself, for instance), if interested in the subject at all, would have postulated that the Shroud was a medieval forgery. That would be relatively easy to test, assuming one could get one's hands on the cloth itself. But the possibility that the Shroud ever could be tested directly was nonexistent in 1974, when Jackson, then twenty-eight years of age, decided to tackle the problem. Many of the men and women who were to join this project were young. It is a historical observation that most major discoveries have been made by young investigators. Part of the reason is that they are too inexperienced to believe that anything is impossible, and as a result they go where most "mature" minds fear to tread. Consequently, they shatter old preconceptions, and knowledge makes a great step forward.

All that Jackson had to work with was a photograph of the Shroud. Millions of people had seen this picture during the preceding three quarters of a century. They looked at it and moved on; Jackson stopped and wondered. Rapidly, he developed a hypothesis that if the Shroud had actually covered a body, then some parts of the body — such as the forehead, nose, and chin — would have been in contact with the linen, but recessed areas — like the eye sockets and neck — probably would have had no direct contact. Assuming that something from the body was responsible for the images on the Shroud (an enormous assumption!), the points of body contact should be most intense, and those farther away from the linen should be fainter. If this were all true, then there should be a Shroud-body distance factor that is mathematically calculable and testable. Theoretical physicists are all mathematicians, and Jackson was a competent mathematician. However, most theorists are hopeless experimentalists, and they depend on other scientists to devise and conduct experiments that will prove or disprove the hypotheses they devise.

Jackson needed some experimentalists to help him move forward, and inquired around the Air Force Weapons Laboratory. He thought that if he found someone to do image-enhancement studies on the photograph, and someone else to make measurements, he would be on his way.

By coincidence, a civilian computer scientist whose fields were image enhancement and computer modeling happened to be working as a consultant to the Air Force at that very time. Don Devan was spending every other week at the Weapons Lab, working on "whited-out" film of nuclear explosions. Atomic shots are so energetic that many of the films, even though taken at ultrahigh speed, show almost nothing but the white of overexposure during the early microseconds of the event. Devan's task was to see whether, by image enhancement, any information could be recovered from the pictures. It was a fairly uninteresting chore.

One day Devan was doggedly working away when Jackson appeared, introduced himself, and asked whether he had ever heard of the Shroud of Turin.

Devan looked at him blankly and replied, "No, what is it?"

Jackson hunkered down and went into the rather complex story of the Shroud, its purported origin, and the hypothesis he wanted to test. Devan had been brought up as an Orthodox Jew — not that that would make any difference to a dedicated scientist like Devan, whose instinctive response to the story was "That sounds interesting. Let's see the photograph."

His first reaction was pure pleasure. Compared with the whited-out material he had been working with, the photograph of the Shroud had lots of information in it. Devan asked the generation of the photograph he was looking at. A copy of an original photograph is second generation; a copy of a copy is third. The farther away from the original, the more likely it is that the copy will have lost definition and picked up adventitious content. Like static on a radio, and throughout science in any system, such irrelevant and unwanted material is called "noise." The relevant information is the signal. The signal-to-noise ratio is a key problem in almost any experimental method that obtains or transmits information. The picture Jackson had was fourth generation and very noisy.

Devan proposed to do microdensitometry on the photograph. A densitometer is a very simple instrument that measures the darkness, or density, of any spot on a film. A microdensitometer looks at a very little spot. Jackson and Devan proceeded to take about 750,000 measurements by hand, one after the other, on their fourth-generation photograph. After all the points were ascertained, they had to be converted into a "language" that the computers could work with. Digital computers have only two pieces of data they can understand: the digits zero and one. All information that is given to a computer must first be digitized. Converting data into a language that can be digested by a computer, along with instructions for what is to be done with it, is the job of programmers. In basic scientific research, investigators do not have the luxury of a battery of programmers to assist them. Each investigator must know appropriate computer language and function as his own programmer, operator, and strategist.

Theoretician Jackson needed computer help, and Rudy Dichtl knew just what kind of colleague he was looking for. The man had to be (1) good as an experimentalist, (2) capable as a computer jockey, (3) able to design and program testable models to examine the validity of a hypothesis, (4) willing to use his own free time for a project that many might consider on or beyond the borderline of responsible, scientific enterprise, (5) interested in the several specific scientific disciplines this work called for, and finally, (6) roused to curiosity by the Shroud of Turin.

By coincidence, a man meeting all of the first five criteria joined the Weapons Lab at that precise time. He was Dr. Eric Jumper.

Jumper was in his twenties and had received his doctorate in engineering. He was, in scientific jargon, a nuts-and-bolts man, a thermodynamicist, and a hard head. This latter term is not derogatory; it refers to a serious-minded man who wants everything reduced from hypothesis to uncompromising, unequivocal data for which statistical evidence is overwhelming. According to Jumper's description of himself at this time in his life, he was relatively unimaginative. The only book he had ever read outside his academic work and his scientific reading was *The Adventures of Sherlock Holmes*. He enjoyed the military, aerodynamics, heat-exchange problems, and tough engineering challenges. He was, and is, forthright, painfully blunt, and undiplomatic, as well as uncompromising in his honesty.

Jackson thought that Jumper might meet the first five criteria, but he was in considerable doubt about the sixth. The theoretician approached the pragmatist, introduced himself, and asked if he was familiar with the Shroud of Turin.

"The what of which?" queried Jumper.

Jackson proceeded to tell him. Jumper stared at him through his metal-rimmed glasses. He looked at the picture, agreed that it was unusual, but said he really was not interested.

Jumper recalls, "I thought it was totally bizarre that anyone would even fantasize that this might not be a painting."

Jackson seldom takes no for an answer. He does not argue with a person, he never twists an arm, but he has a way of beating one on the head with an eiderdown club of earnest words, and he seems never to let up. In desperation, almost anyone will agree to nearly anything, if only to get him to stop.

Jackson gave Barbet's book about the Shroud to Jumper and told him he should read it. At first blush, there seems to be no connection between Barbet and Conan Doyle, but both authors had one thing in common — they wrote about mysteries. Jumper took a quick browse and was astonished to find that Barbet thought the Shroud was authentic. Of course, Barbet was a physician, not a scientist, and Jumper understood the difference. Nonetheless, he decided to read the book, and was appalled by the *Schrecklichkeit*. Though he had seen many crucifixes, he recalls, "I always thought they were sort of beautiful: an almost effeminate man, without a hairy chest, who does not look as if he's in too much pain — almost a glorifying thing. When I read Barbet, I was shocked by the horror of his gruesome, long, medical description of the crucifixion. I still didn't think the Shroud was authentic, but I thought I might be a little interested in what John and Don Devan were doing. I was sure, however, that I wasn't going to tag along with them. I returned the Barbet book to John and told him I thought it was sort of interesting."

Jackson smiled and said, "That's what I've been trying to tell you."

They both met with Devan, who suspected that there might be something in the Shroud-body distance hypothesis, but was concerned that the 35-mm film they were using was too noisy. He wanted a better photograph. The three men checked and found that the film came from an organization called the Holy Shroud Guild, the president of which was Father Adam Otterbein. They drafted a letter describing what they were doing and asking the priest whether they could obtain any better, earlier-generation pictures.

When the Holy Shroud Guild was formed, in 1959, its twin purposes were to propagate knowledge about the subject and to support learned investigation into the Shroud. Father Otterbein had been appointed as the guild's first president. For years, he had been trying to foster scientific interest in the artifact. So far he had obtained opinions from but one group — forensic pathologists. Some had agreed to read Barbet and check his conclusions against their own knowledge. Barbet had been a battlefield surgeon in World War I. As such, he had probably seen more wounds, and the imprints they make on bandages, than most physicians see in a lifetime. Barbet claimed that in all the European art he had ever seen, ranging from that of the Renaissance to paintings from the modern era, he had never seen an accurate rendering of either wounds or the appearance of blood on cloth dressings. In contrast, he claimed, the Shroud was accurate in every particular. The forensic pathologists whose work on the Shroud has been published agree with Barbet on this point.

Father Otterbein, however, wanted scientific — as opposed to medical — opinion. He approached numerous forensic scientists who agreed to look into the problem, provided the priest would give them the Shroud to examine. Needless to say, this left the cleric frustrated and more than a mite exasperated, because the Shroud was taken out of its sanctuary only a few times each century. Thus, when he heard from some highly qualified scientists who merely wanted a *better photograph,* he complied at once and sent off a second-generation film made from an original 1931 picture. Jackson, Devan, and Jumper received it with delight. Devan and Jumper began doing microdensitometric studies of the new film in the Weapons Laboratory. Devan would take the microdensitometer readings, and, late at night, in their spare time, Jackson and Jumper would write programs for the giant computer. The computer would crunch out data, spitting out reams of print-out material on which presumably were the forehead, nose, chin, thorax, hands, and knee data encrypted in alpha-numeric code (letters and numbers). When this paper was laid out flat, there should have been a reproduction of the Shroud logged in the alpha-numeric pattern. They could almost recognize it — perhaps and maybe. But the noise was so great that the "perhaps" had a big question mark after it. Devan and Jumper, joined by Rudy Dichtl, were trying to milk the data for all they were worth — and were having fun.

Meanwhile, Jackson's grasshopper mind was never still. His troops were working on one problem, so he zipped off to create another. He wanted to find a model of a crucified man to make measurements to see if he could clarify some of the noisy alpha-numeric data. He took a small wall cross with a crucified Christ on it, and with string tried to make some measurements of distances between high points. Theoretical physicists sometimes propose experiments that are weird to an experimentalist.

Jumper, when he finally paused long enough to listen to the theoretician with his little crucifix and string, just snorted. "If you want to make an analogy to the real world, let's do it with real people, not wall decorations."

Dichtl began to search for volunteers whose height and physique were similar to those of the man on the Shroud. After some had been recruited, each was placed on his back in an anatomic position as close as possible to that represented on the cloth, and was photographed with a fixed camera and measured. He was then covered with a sheet, rephotographed, and remeasured. All the information was digitized, and the computer began to crunch out more numbers. As these read-outs were compared with the digitized Shroud numbers, it became apparent that there was more than a casual relationship between them, but the noisiness of the Shroud image did not permit a firm conclusion. While Jumper wrestled with this problem, Jackson, who now had three people involved in what Jumper describes appropriately as the dog work, decided to follow a clue that might get others involved. He did not then realize that one of his great talents was in being a scientific Pied Piper: he would play his Shroud flute, and the researchers would fall in behind him.

The largest sponsor of the Jet Propulsion Laboratory, the huge enterprise under the aegis of Cal Tech, is NASA. The JPL is responsible for those superb space photographs of the planets, their moons, surfaces, and rings which are justly famous. These photographs travel through space as extremely tiny electrical impulses, some as small as a femtowatt (10^{-18} watts or 1/1,000,000,000,000,000,000th of a watt). They are picked out of space by massive antennae and are then processed through highly complex electronic arrays that must cope with the signal-to-noise problem. They finally appear, bit by bit, on receivers, and at that point, image-enhancement specialists go to work to obtain the optimal image with a minimum of noise. All of these specialists admit that in order to accomplish their mission, they must be first-rate computer jockeys who, in addition to relying on mathematics and physics, must employ a degree of "black art." Black art is a combination of human intelligence, technique, the ability to perceive almost subliminal stimuli, common sense, experience, and intuition. Black art is a talent that the image-enhancement specialists at the JPL possess in abundance.

Jackson had earlier met two key scientists on the Viking project at the JPL, and he now realized that they could be of considerable use. He flew to Los Angeles, and by the time he returned, he had Don Lynn and Jean Lorre hooked on the Shroud problem. He left with them copies of the second-generation film so that they could exercise their science and craft.

Father Otterbein of the Holy Shroud Guild had in his possession some Kodachromes that he had taken in 1973, the last time the Shroud had been removed from its sanctuary in the cathedral and exhibited. The apparatus that keeps it within the vault where it is kept was designed to be thief-proof, tamper-proof, and people-proof. The mechanism resembles an insane inventor's version of the boiler room of the *Queen Mary*. In 1973, the previous archbishop-cardinal and the former king of Italy, who is the legal owner of the Shroud, decided to unveil the cloth for its television debut. Among the few privileged to be present were the president of the Holy Shroud Guild, Father Otterbein, and the vice president, Father Peter Rinaldi. Naturally, the two clerics were taking photographs as fast as their fingers could cock and press a shutter release. When Jackson received copies of these Kodachromes, he wondered what could be learned from the colored photographs that could not be gleaned from the black and white 1931 film.

Knowing very little about color, he began to ask questions of every scientist he could reach at the Weapons Lab. He realized that filters would have to be used if he was to obtain some basic information, and was told that Wratten filters were the best choice. Jackson had no idea what a Wratten filter was, but that did not deter him. Indeed, nothing seems to phase Jackson when he is locked into a problem that fascinates him. He started a search for the filters. The Weapons Lab is complex, huge, and magnificently equipped, but it seemed that there simply were no Wratten filters available.

Jackson decided to send copies of the color film to Lynn and Lorre at the JPL. Don Lynn, who was the supervisor of the Space Processing Group, never considered himself to be "overly religious." It was late in 1975, and Lynn and his crew were preparing for the Viking landing on Mars. Any idea of a nine-to-five day goes out the window when "events" take place at the JPL. Somehow, in the microcracks of time that occurred now and again, Lorre and Lynn squeezed out some work on the Shroud. They looked at the pictures, and their eyes and brains told them what it was. They had the computer look at the photos, and that was a different story.

The human brain is a marvelous machine. This may seem so obvious as to be a cliché. It is not. It is a source of wonder to any thoughtful scientist or philosopher. It is a source of frustration to those who use their own brains and try to create artificial intelligence in computers. Thus, when man looks at a photo of the Shroud, he sees a man with wounds. When a computer "looks" at a picture of the Shroud, it "sees" something vaguely like a human image, but it also sees a huge amount of extraneous material that detracts from the man. Our brains will instantly sort out and reject extraneous material and focus on the human figure and its significance. A computer works differently; ordered to "look," it will see everything. If we want a computer to ignore all irrelevant material, we try to structure some mathematical device — an algorithm (which may not be possible) — that can tell the computer, in mathematical terms, what to ignore and what to register — always assuming that we know what these parameters are.

To comprehend completely the computer's problems with the photograph, we need to recall an important bit of history. In 1532, the Shroud was in a silver casket that was kept in a sanctuary built of wood and stone. A *torchère,* which was carelessly left burning after vespers, burned down and kindled the wooden wall. As the flames crept up, the fire spread across the rafters, and soon the entire structure was aflame. The silver casket began to get hot; then fiery wood embers fell on top of it, burning fiercely. Some people sleeping nearby awoke and rushed to the blazing building, picking up buckets of water as they ran. They threw open the doors of the sanctuary, which caused huge drafts of air to fan the growing inferno above the box to a heat of around 900°C — the temperature at which the impure medieval silver is known to melt. Areas of the top of the casket became white hot and then melted. The molten drops of silver fell into the casket, burning their way through the folded linen and puddling at the bottom. Fortunately, the container was small and tight, so only a little oxygen was available and the linen could not burst into flame. The men ran to save the cloth. Hooking it free from the pyre must have been a heroic act, for the flames were so intense that the building was destroyed. The box, with glowing silver spots, was doused with water. With a great hissing, the receptacle was quenched, and the heated water was sucked into the holes on top — where the silver had melted away — by the vacuum produced inside by the sudden reduction of temperature. The ruined reliquary was taken out and opened, and the charred, perforated, and partly sodden Shroud was removed. The rescuers were apparently awed when they realized that the holes and scorch marks were on both sides of the image, running almost the length of the Shroud, but that the image of the man was virtually untouched. They undoubtedly suspected divine intercession. The water stains had made large, ugly, bilaterally symmetrical blotches on the material; nothing could be done about them. The holes were patched with Holland cloth — another type of linen — from various sources. These patches of different origins can easily be seen in photographs of the Shroud.

The Shroud itself has been folded so many times that wrinkles have formed at the fold lines, and these are also very obvious on the film. The margins of several major water stains intersect nearly every other feature. There are also some random burn holes that were apparently not made at the time of the 1532 fire. The origin of these peculiar burn holes is murky, at best. In the often lurid, sometimes accurate, and frequently fanciful histories of the cloth, it is difficult to sort out truth from fiction. For example, one account states that hot rods of iron had been poked through the cloth to prove its authenticity. To understand that, one must be able to enter the mind of the fourteenth-century religious — which is certainly beyond my ability. This yarn may account for the other burn holes. Those old accounts which talk of hot iron pokers also state that the cloth was boiled in oil to prove its authenticity. This also seems to me a strange authentication method. In addition, there are variations in the diameter of the individual hand-spun threads used in the weaving, which leave patterns of different shades of color on the film. There are smudges, dirt, specks, blotches, flecks, wrinkles, bulges, and valleys, as well as the underlying herringbone weave.

All of this extraneous material is subtracted by man's brain as he glances at a picture of the Shroud and recognizes at once that these are human images. A computer will look at the same film of the Shroud and see everything without discrimination. That is what makes the images so noisy. Every time scientists try to instruct the computer to subtract some of the noise, they find that the images lose definition. And this is what makes image enhancement an art. When those femtowatt signals come in from space probes like Mariner, Viking, or Voyager, they are accompanied by the cosmic static of the universe, especially of our galaxy. It is this noise which must be extracted at the JPL so that clear pictures of planetary surfaces can be had. The photographs of the Shroud presented a similar dilemma.

In the wee hours of one morning, Lynn and Lorre sat down and asked themselves what they should do about the Shroud project. They finally realized that they did not know what others in the group wanted to learn from the film. When Lynn had asked Jackson, he was told, "Anything you can find out." Essentially, they had the responsibility of asking themselves what other people should or might want to know, and obtaining answers where possible.

Deciding that a clearer picture was needed, they resolved to try to clean the film by getting rid of the noise. But then they ran into the kind of situation that plagues this type of endeavor.

As Lynn remembers, "Cleaning up the film didn't work too well, because there was such a spectrum of intensities in it, from burns, noise, the body, and the blood, that when you took out noise, you took out data."

This was exactly what Devan and Jumper had concluded back in Albuquerque. Lorre suggested that they go at the problem the other way around. If, he reasoned, they were getting nowhere by trying to improve the images cosmetically, and hence obtaining more information about what they were, they could try to find out what the images were not.

Lynn formulated the problem: "It's obvious that the first and perhaps key question is 'Can these be paintings?' That ought to be easy. We'll do a power spectrum and Fourier transform of the images." These are mathematical manipulations, and these they proceeded to do.

"Other than DC, there weren't any frequency spectra — none. Any brush strokes of a painting must leave some specific frequencies and directions. You can have several or many different directions. But you can't expect absolute randomness, and that's exactly what we found."

Any artist, be he right- or left-handed, must have a direction in his brush marks when he puts on color. Even if it is up and down, as in the paintings of the Pointillists, there is a direction. But on the Shroud there was none. Clearly, the images were not oil paintings or water colors on top of cloth made by brush.

The conclusion by the JPL group that the images were directionless certainly tended to injure the forgery hypothesis. It was not a fatal wound, by any means, but it played ducks and drakes with my assumption that the chances were better than 95 percent that the Shroud was a forgery.

Lynn managed to clear up the computer image somewhat, though he thought he could have done so more easily by hand with a pencil eraser than with a computer. Computers can set a man on the moon or plot an intercept course on an incoming missile in microseconds. Yet here, with the most sophisticated hardware and software, a top computer jockey thought he could have done a better job with a pencil eraser. It gladdens the spirit of the humanist within us — even scientists.

Lynn and Lorre did some enhancement, and Lynn later recalled: "Relics have always turned me off. I just reject them out of hand. I was extremely skeptical, but as some early data began to emerge, a thought that I kept at the outermost limit of my mind was saying, 'Wouldn't this be incredible if it really might be . . .' Then I'd shut it out and wait for developments. After they came along, I'd fan the flame of my skepticism. It became a game of let's see how we can shoot this one down."

Actually, this "game" was indulged in by each team member — not only in his own thoughts, but in letters to one another, phone calls, conferences, and rap sessions. The entire subject matter was bound to be controversial. If any of the observations or conclusions were wrong, each wanted to be the first to find out about it. The team members challenged themselves and one another. From time to time they would trade sides in a discussion. It would be far better to find chinks in their armor of data as they progressed, rather than have others do it later.

However, Don Lynn was in a better position than many

others. He had worked on the Mariner missions to Venus
and Mercury, and on Viking and then Voyager to Jupiter,
Saturn, and beyond. He had seen all kinds of long-held
scientific theories about our planetary system shot down,
and emergence of dramatic new discoveries from the microscopic to the astronomic. Science, in the last quarter of the
twentieth century, is totally alien in one sense from the linear or even exponential growth avenues of the past. Quali-
tatively and quantitatively, the rate of new discovery, techniques, and knowledge is on an asymptotic curve. It seems
to go straight up, with no end in sight. We have learned
more in one space shot than in several centuries of tele-
scopic observation. Even greater leaps are occurring in biology and cosmology. The boundaries where chemistry begins and physics or biology leave off have been replaced by
a continuum. Why assume that classical boundaries con-
strain us on a subject such as the Shroud? And, incidentally, what is the name of this subject?

As an object of scientific research, the Shroud contains an
incredible number of diverse ingredients, which fall into
many different categories of knowledge. It is made of linen,
which comes from the flax plant — botany. The fiber made
from flax is a polysaccharide, meaning that it is a biological
polymer of sugar, which is a carbohydrate. So we have
biopolymers, carbohydrate chemistry, or polysaccharide
chemistry. Converting the flax plant into linen fibers to be
spun and woven is textile technology.

The linen bears the images, front and back, of what appears to be a man. The images are straw-yellow. Colors that
are applied by man include those from the sea, like octopus
ink and dyes from mollusks — marine biology and biochemistry; from insects, like cochineal — entomological
biochemistry; from plants, like indigo — botanical biochemistry. Other colors are derived from such elemental salts as
arsenic, copper, and iron — inorganic chemistry. Still others are in the category of organic chemistry.

To determine what kinds of colors something may be

made of, we require a background in physics, including nuclear physics, optics, atomic and molecular physics, and must employ such devices and techniques as ultraviolet, visible and infrared spectrophotometry, atomic absorption spectroscopy, neutron activation, nuclear magnetic resonance, mass spectroscopy, electron microprobe, X-ray diffraction, and on and on. Colors are applied in liquid form in aqueous dilution using "vehicles" like gelatin (proteins from animals), albumins (proteins from eggs), lipids (oils, fats, and waxes from vegetable and animal sources). These bring in the fields of protein and polypeptide chemistry, lipid chemistry, and even some petroleum chemistry. The images of the man may be realistic — human anthropology; and his apparent wounds may have verisimilitude — physiology, pathophysiology, forensic pathology, medicine, biology. The ostensible blood may be real — hematology, porphyrin chemistry, biochemistry, spectrometry, immunology. The image may have been imprinted on the fabric by physical means — radiation physics, molecular transport — which call on physical chemistry, thermodynamics, kinetics. These would involve pyrolysis chemistry, and determining the water stains would require chromatography. Pollens and micro-organisms on the cloth involve knowledge of palynology, bacteriology, and mycology. We would need to invoke mathematics as well as computer science in order to construct models of the images.

This is not a complete list, and is written only in hindsight. No one on the team had any idea of the diversity of scientific disciplines that this project would demand. Initially, most of the investigators came from the physical sciences. Jackson was trained in theoretical physics; Jumper, in engineering and thermodynamics. Most scientists are trained in a single discipline. Others, whose curiosity mandates it, are trained across disciplinary boundaries. In this quest, nearly all of us had to learn other disciplines to some degree. We had to call on experts in scores of areas, such as art history, mores, customs, techniques of ancients, paleoclimatology, volcanology, and archeochemistry — for example. We not only had to learn new areas, but then had to check and recheck, and check once more our new perceptions, knowledge, and insights with those of our colleagues at many universities and government and industrial laboratories, here and abroad.

Many of us were at first quite confident of our technical adequacy. Some may have even been cocky. But none of us survived this extraordinary voyage into the unknown without becoming more humble and more aware of the dimensions of our ignorance. Scientific hubris may have been our mutual sin at the outset. Now we have learned better.

Don Lynn and Jean Lorre were sitting on the most powerful battery of image-analysis hardware and software in the history of man, and there was no quick and easy way to use it to apply to the images on the Shroud.

While the JPL men were puzzling about how to treat the Shroud, Jackson, back in New Mexico, was also wondering about the color and still looking for Wratten filters. Finally, someone suggested that Sandia Laboratory might have some. Sandia, in Albuquerque, is another government facility that handles much top-secret material. Like a hound dog on a scent, Jackson made contact with Bill Mottern, a Sandia physicist. Mottern had a set of Wrattens, but he had something else as well. That "something," by coincidence, put the whole project into global high gear. It was a VP-8.

The VP-8 image analyzer has at its heart a computer. It was designed for the space program. Everyone has seen the magnificent pictures of the planets obtained by NASA. The space probes do not carry cameras in the common sense of the word. They have a device that picks up light signals electronically and transmits them to earth. Recall a picture of Saturn with its rings. The portions of the rings closest to the probe are brighter. Those parts of the rings which go behind the planet show less light; they are darker. The VP-8 is so programmed that it interprets "darker" as farther away. It can take the signals coming in from Saturn, for example, and show them on its television screen as a 3-D picture of a planet. In contrast, let us take a picture of a man whose face is illuminated from a light to the right of him. The left part of his face is in some shadow. Put this photograph in the VP-8, and you will see a grossly distorted face, with the darker part of the countenance farther away and the bright part in the forefront. Indeed, any photograph of a man or a statue or a landscape — which are, after all, flat or 2-D — results in a badly contorted image on the VP-8 screen. It is only when *actual* depth or remoteness is shown by less light that the VP-8 can produce a 3-D picture. The description of "less or more light" depends on the number of quanta or photons of light.

Jackson had never heard of a VP-8, but when he drove over to Sandia, he took photos of the Shroud with him. Mottern asked him why he wanted to use the Wratten filters. Jackson, always ready to chat about his baby, launched into the story of the Shroud. Obligingly, the Sandia scientist brought out the filters. And then he put forward a really dumb idea.

"Why," he suggested, "don't we put the photos of the Shroud into the VP-8?"

Never loath to try a new idea, Jackson agreed.

All in all, it should have been a stupid waste of time, for a flat photo will, and can, give only a warped picture.

They placed the Shroud photo in the VP-8 and twiddled the dials, focus, and rotation. Suddenly, both men saw, swimming up from the electronic fog of the screen, a perfect three-dimensional image of a scourged, crucified man.

Impossible! Ridiculous! Outrageous! Yes. But it was there. The two scientists just stared.

The positive photograph of the man in the Shroud had the appearance of a two-dimensional face. The VP-8's three-dimensional image was as stunningly different from the photograph as a statue is from a painting. The long hair, full beard and mustache, the serenity on the face of a badly battered, crucified man, came alive, giving Jackson and Mottern the eerie impression that they were gazing at an actual face of a man, not at a painting or a sculpture.

Finally, Jackson took a deep breath. "Bill," he said, "do you realize that we may be the first people in two thousand years who know exactly how Christ looked in the tomb?"

John Jackson is normally soft-spoken, and his strongest expletive is "gosh." Yet on this day, as he was driving back to Albuquerque, he had to give vent to his emotion. He yelled his cry for the pinnacle of exultant excitement: "Yabba-dabba-doo!"

When he first told me of this event, I asked, "Yabba-dabba-doo? John! That's what a seven-year-old might say when given a giant Tootsie Roll. Is that the top of your euphoric vocabulary?"

He twinkled as he smiled at me and said, "Yes. That's the biggest and the best."

3

Can We Test the Real Thing?

WHEN, at nightfall, Jackson arrived back home, he found that he was to baby-sit that night, because his wife was going to a meeting. Otherwise, he would have roared over to Eric Jumper's house to show him the 3-D photographs that he and Mottern had taken of the man in the Shroud from the cathode ray tube of the VP-8. Since he couldn't, he called his colleague, only to find that Jumper was also baby-sitting.

"Eric," said Jackson, "you're not going to believe this."

After describing the VP-8 and how it worked, he then described the picture in front of him. "Eric, I'm looking at a perfect 3-D body shape. It's as lifelike as you can possibly imagine."

Eric nearly crawled through the telephone.

The next day, first thing, Jumper came to Jackson's office with his hand outstretched. When he was given the photographs, he became utterly still and stared and stared. Finally, he whirled on his heel and ran out of the office, followed by Jackson. He stopped everyone he saw in the corridor, and said, "Hey, look! Look at this! Take a look! What do you think!"

Officer-scientists came crowding out of their offices and clustered around, exclaiming.

Jackson thought, "Oh, man, I'm obviously *not* crazy. Look at Eric and all these other scientists getting excited. I'm not the only one who's nuts."

Those momentous 3-D photographs pretty well torpedoed the rest of the day for the young physical scientists. Eric was delighted, because the pictures were confirmation to him that all the tough, tedious, time-consuming work on the Shroud-body distance problem was correct. With one dumb experiment, which was to be epochal, Jackson had a tool — 3-D photos — that were to transform his hobby into a project.

No longer did one have to be a mathematician or a physicist to understand alpha-numeric computer print-outs. Now he had pictures that were worth a thousand words — or even chapters. As he was basking in the glow of comprehension and sympathetic understanding of other scientists, he suddenly remembered that Father Otterbein was due to arrive that evening to spend a few days with him and see what these Air Force scientists had been doing with the photographs he had supplied.

When the priest arrived and had greeted the family, Jackson sat him down and began to talk. He showed Father Otterbein the VP-8 picture and sat back, expecting an explosive reaction. The priest just smiled and said that it was nice, but he had seen it before. Jackson was thunderstruck; he could not believe his ears. What the priest thought he was seeing was a photo of a touched-up carving. Others, in the past, had projected the picture on plaster or wood and tried to carve a 3-D rendering of the 2-D image.

Jackson realized that he was not explaining clearly what the pictures were, so he began at the beginning. He talked about intensity versus vertical distance, digitized pictures, gamma enhancement, microdensitometers, plots, digital data, alpha-numeric symbols, computer plots, hand-drawn plots, signal-to-noise ratios, and on and on, into the dawn. Father Otterbein, whose training was in theology and the humanities, tuned out by the third sentence. However, he smiled and nodded as the theoretical physicist droned on into the night. Later, Jackson recalled that he thought that the priest was pretty "cool" about all the information. In point of fact, he was not cool; he was stupefied.

The next day he was whisked off to Sandia to get a crash course on the VP-8, optics, physics, mathematics, and computer graphics. Then back to the Jackson house for another all-night session. Father Otterbein was drowning.

The following day Jumper saw that the priest looked punch-drunk. Knowing Jackson's proclivity for talking, and imagining how he indulged it if he had a captive audience, Jumper arranged for the priest to come to his house for a couple of days.

"Thank God," said Father Otterbein as he arrived at the Jumpers'. "I couldn't have taken another night. I have a heart condition, and I still don't know what he's talking about." After he had had a few days of rest, Jumper explained in plain English what Jackson had been trying to communicate, and finally the light began to dawn for the bewildered priest. This insight was to have far-reaching consequences.

A short while later, Jackson received orders transferring him to the faculty of the Air Force Academy in Colorado Springs. He said good-bye to Jumper, Dichtl, Devan, and Mottern. He realized that, with his collaborators gone and his chance to use the VP-8 removed by several hundred mountainous miles, his work on the Shroud was finished for some time to come. He had not reckoned, however, on that marvelously ubiquitous property which helped this research project through so many impasses — coincidence.

In the Marines, an odd event occurring once is random chance, twice is coincidence, three times is enemy action. Had the Marines been involved in the Shroud project, the prevalence of coincidence would have convinced them that our galaxy was being invaded.

Ten days after the Jacksons had settled into their new house in Colorado Springs, there was a knock on the door.

Opening it, John saw Eric, who smiled and said, "Guess what, good buddy. I've just been transferred to the academy, too."

Chance now struck again. Shortly before he left the Weapons Lab, Jackson had decided to take a course of special study at another institution. There he met Dr. Robert Dinegar, a physical chemist from Los Alamos. While chatting with Dinegar, he mentioned the Shroud and, with his nose constantly aquiver for new colleagues, asked whether there were any scientists at Los Alamos who might be interested in some of the scientific problems raised by the cloth. Dinegar immediately thought of several, including himself. He offered to round them up if Jackson would come to the laboratory to talk about the Shroud. Jackson agreed. The meeting was held, and still another group was added to the team.

In the meantime, Father Otterbein realized that for the first time since he had assumed the leadership of the Holy Shroud Guild, he had found some honest-to-goodness card-carrying scientists who were interested in one of the two objectives of his mandate: scholarly investigation into the subject of the Shroud. He had, naturally, run into large numbers of people from the lunatic fringe of humanity, who really must be experienced to be believed. Though always courteous, the priest had learned how to distinguish the sheep from the nuts. For some time he had had a dream, one that he shared only with Father Rinaldi, the vice president of the guild. Both men were thinking ahead to 1978, when the Shroud was to be exhibited to the public in celebration of the four-hundredth anniversary of its arrival in Turin. The priests were hoping that, at some point between the end of the exhibition and the linen's return to its sanctuary, the American scientists would be permitted to examine it. Unlike Father Otterbein, Father Rinaldi had a parish, in New Rochelle, New York. He was born in Turin and as a youth had served as an altar boy in the cathedral where the Shroud was kept. There he learned all about the

Shroud — the Santa Sindone. After becoming a priest, he was transferred from Turin to New York State, but he had never lost his interest in the Holy Shroud of Turin, and, in fact, had written two books on the subject. An extraordinarily warm and handsome man, with a shock of white hair, Rinaldi is immediately commanding when he walks into any gathering. His interest had brought him and Adam Otterbein together. They began to plan for 1978.

Father Rinaldi had maintained close contact with many Turinese in key positions in different groups, all of whom had some interest in the Shroud. He traveled back and forth to Italy several times during this period.

While the priests were planning, Jackson and Jumper had a brainstorm. It suddenly occurred to them that there were now so many people involved in the Shroud project that they should call for a scientific conference in order to present scientific reports so that ideas could be exchanged. In short, they decided to convoke a scientific colloquium. Colloquia are expensive. At the very minimum, there is the rent for an auditorium, screens, projectors, blackboard, overhead viewers, and other equipment. The costs of travel, room, and board for the participants must be defrayed by some third party. They are usually underwritten by a scientific society, industrial sponsors who wish to publicize their products, foundations, private and public granting agencies, universities, or similar institutions.

In this case, none of the above was at hand. There was no money. None for travel of the scientists to and from the meeting site. There was none for invitations, telephone calls, or the printing of the proceedings of the conference after it was concluded. The whole idea was daft. However, daft ideas were becoming Jackson's forte.

At that time, five thousand miles away in England, another coincidence was taking shape. A British film producer, David Rolf, decided to make a docudrama about the Shroud. He had heard through the British Holy Shroud Guild, who had the word from its American counterpart, that some scientists in the United States were doing some extremely intriguing work on the subject. Rolf called Jackson and Jumper. Would they be willing to appear in the film and explain what they were doing? Certainly! Why not?

In 1977, Rolf arrived at the Air Force Academy. Jackson, Jumper, and Lynn, who had come from Los Angeles for the occasion, made their film debut in a one-hour film entitled *The Silent Witness*. To their complete surprise, the three men received a total of $2000 for their appearances.

Jackson grinned at Jumper and said, "Eric, we have our meeting financed."

It was to be held on a weekend. Most Shroud meetings would be on weekends so as not to interfere with anyone's work-a-day activity. The meeting was to turn out to be absolutely pivotal for the entire future of the Shroud research project. As the idea for the Albuquerque meeting took form, Fathers Otterbein and Rinaldi decided that the time had come to take Jackson into their confidence.

Father Otterbein called Jackson. "You know," he said, "there's a chance — but only a remote one — that you people may be permitted to observe the Shroud itself, after it's publicly exhibited in 1978. But don't get your hopes up."

Jackson, however, took off like a scalded cat. As far as he was concerned, even the tiniest possibility was the opportunity of a lifetime. He knew the Shroud was taken out of its reliquary only a few times each century. From here on, he wanted everyone involved to think in terms of a 1978 deadline and have the strongest possible scientific case so that the chance of "hands-on" testing would be as great as could be. He and Jumper rushed to the telephone and began calling all their teammates to alert them to the possibility. Now the scientific colloquium took on a special urgency. This would not be a general session. There would be formal papers presented. Everyone would caucus and construct a protocol of experiments to be done if the opportunity arose to do actual testing. Jackson reasoned that a rigorous, intelligent, positive proposal would be the most effective means of persuading those in authority to agree.

When Devan received the news, he could not at first believe it. As it began to sink in, he suddenly realized that, although the team had some talent and capability in image enhancement, not one member was a photographer. Devan himself had taken fewer than ten pictures in his lifetime, and did not own a camera. He called Jumper and told him that he had a connection that might produce the desired photographer.

Eric snapped, "Go!"

Devan picked up the phone and called Barrie Schwortz, a man he had worked with some years back, who was a professional photographer and a graduate of the prestigious Brooks Institute of Photography in Santa Barbara.

Schwortz told Devan that he was not the one to do the scientific photography. However, he would love to do the documentary photography. He recommended Vern Miller, a faculty member of the Brooks Institute whose specialty was the technical and scientific use of photography, and a meeting was set up.

Through Vern Miller, Devan inducted the head of the institute, Ernest Brooks, and an optical physicist-spectroscopist named Sam Pellicori, who worked at a research institute in Santa Barbara. Don Devan became the coordinator and the point man for the whole photographic effort, which turned out to be one of the most massive projects undertaken. Vern Miller, with his assistant Mark Evans, Barrie Schwortz, Ernie Brooks, and Sam Pellicori, would together take between five thousand and seven thousand photographs; the exact number has never been counted. The amount of preparation for this project alone was intense and complicated. Entire camera support systems had to be built. In addition to ordinary filters, special liquid filters, containing certain chemicals to be placed over lights, had to be constructed. Known fluors and absorbers had to be tested. Narrow-band filters for the entire range from infrared through the visible spectrum down to the ultraviolet had to be prepared. In addition, set-ups were needed for photo-microscopy. If permission was granted for team members to go to Turin to test the Shroud, nobody had any idea where the examination would take place. In circumstances like those, the best plan is to assume that the worst case will occur. The worst case for photomicroscopy is that there will be a lot of vibration. The slightest tremor in the micro-scope, the camera, the support system, or the object being photographed can ruin the results. Vibration usually comes through the floor — but not always. The system must be so cushioned and buffered that most of the vibratory interfer-ence can be dampened. The problem is analogous to de-signing a workable photographic system that will be per-fectly stable in the middle of a moderate earthquake. This is hardly an overstatement, for ostensibly minor vibrations underfoot are greatly magnified in the photomicroscopic system. A 50 X micrograph will result in at least a fiftyfold amplification of any vibration.

Once the photographers had dealt with the vibration problem, they had to create a system whereby the entire rig could travel with great stability back and forth over a four-teen-foot length, and up and down over a three-and-a-half-foot width, so that any single area of fabric or image could be microphotographed. At the same time, whatever rig would support the Shroud itself also needed to be oscilla-tion-proof, or at least oscillation-resistant.

Then there was the challenge of lighting, and they had no notion about the type of room that would be available. Would the walls and ceiling be reflective or absorbing? Would there be windows? If so, how could the light be blocked out for infrared photography? (Black plastic, for ex-ample, if placed over windows may cause a complete black-out as far as our eyes are concerned. Nonetheless, it is al-most transparent to infrared streaming in.) If there were windows, how many? What area would they cover? What kind of temporary building materials could they bring that would make a well-windowed room completely light-tight?

And, finally, where, oh where, would they be able to find an appropriate microscope for this peculiar application?

Similar plans were being made by other groups involved in the project in preparation for the Albuquerque meeting.

As Devan recalls: "It was one of the strangest conferences I have ever been at in my life. The first thing that was odd was that you could divide the room about down the middle between clerics and scientists."

In addition to Fathers Otterbein and Rinaldi, the clergy included a monsignor from Rome, an Anglican priest from London, a Jesuit professor of theology from Loyola University in Chicago, and, the most prestigious of the lot, the Right Reverend Dr. John A. T. Robinson, a bishop and dean of Trinity College, Cambridge. Robinson, a leading Protestant New Testament theologian and author, is held in extremely high regard by many faculty members of United States seminaries. He had become aware of Jackson and Jumper's work on the Shroud — especially the VP-8 work — and as a result, had apparently made a 180-degree turn away from his previous position of skepticism. He was willing to regard the Shroud as a silent witness to the events in the Gospels. Ian Wilson had come over from England, and there were two others present who would play a significant role in the days ahead — Harry and Erica John of the De Rance Foundation.

Devan continues: "This conference was the first that I had ever been at, out of many, where no one was saying, 'Do it my way!' People actually began to say 'I'll tell you what; I think your approach to that problem is better than mine — I'll help you.' I was amazed at the level of cooperation that began to emerge from that meeting. People were actually willing to get off their pet area of expertise and participate as a technician or a bottle polisher to help someone else's experiment go. It was totally unreal — the level of integrity and cooperation. It was really exhilarating."

Eric Jumper says, "This was really the most wonderful meeting I had ever been at. It was a fun thing."

In the four years I have known Eric Jumper, I have never known him to wax that lyrical about anything. Normally, he is as emotional as a hammer.

On the second day of the meeting, the scientists caucused and worked out a structure for the experimental protocols they would follow if the chance to do actual testing came about.

At this point, Harry John of the De Rance Foundation first interceded in the project. He had been much impressed by the men and the presentations at Albuquerque, and realized that they were operating with their own funds. He volunteered to finance the compilation and printing of all the papers. They were put together in record time and were bound into a 243-page book entitled *Proceedings of the U.S. Conference on the Shroud of Turin.* As soon as it arrived from the printer, Fathers Otterbein and Rinaldi dropped another firecracker into the barrel.

Said Father Otterbein, "You know, John and Eric, Father Rinaldi and I think it would be a good idea if you and some other team members flew over to Turin for a few days. You could take several copies of the *Proceedings* with you, and you could present your research proposals to the Turinese authorities. Incidentally, the De Rance Foundation will cover the cost."

Jackson and Jumper usually are never at a loss for words. This time they were. They chose a few of the key investigators who they thought would be good support, found out who could obtain a short leave from work, and reported back to Father Otterbein that they were ready to go.

"Who," asked Jackson of Adam Otterbein, "are we going to make our presentation to, and do you have any words of advice?"

"No advice," replied the priest. "Just present it in your own words. I'll be there, and Father Rinaldi will translate. The presentation is going to be made to the Centro di Sindonologia."

*

The Centro di Sindonologia — the Center for Shroud Studies — is the child of the four-hundred-year-old Confraternity of the Holy Shroud. Like many things Italian, it was far
from a simple organization. I am not sure that I comprehend to this day the implications of an Italian confraternity,
but essentially it was a group of clerics, of high and low
estate, and laymen who have an interest in the Shroud. It
has never had any official standing in regard to the owner-
ship or disposition of the Shroud, but it certainly has what
it regards as a proprietary interest. The Shroud is owned
now — as it has been for over four hundred years — by the
House of Savoy, the royal house of Italy. Originally, Savoy
held part of France and the Piedmont. In 1578, the Shroud
was transferred to Turin, where it has remained. When
Umberto II, the last king of the Italians, left Italy in 1946,
he did so voluntarily. He never abdicated, nor was he de-
posed. His official status is in official limbo, since it was
never officially defined. In Italy, the word "official" is in-
ordinately important.

The Shroud is kept in the Cathedral of St. John in Turin,
and the archbishop-cardinal of Turin holds the key to one
of the three locks of the reliquary in which it is stored. The
representative of the king has the second key. The canon of
the cathedral and the custodian of the Shroud have the third
key. All three keys must be used to get at the Shroud itself.

Virtually ignoring this official reality, the confraternity set
up a daughter organization in the 1950s — the Centro di
Sindonologia. In the mandate of creation of the Centro, the
confraternity stated that it would be empowered to conduct
research on the Shroud and to do all things necessary to
see that the reputation of the Shroud was never be-
smirched.

I imagine that the only research that was being considered in the 1950s was literary, retrospective, theological,
and historical. The Centro eventually published a small pe-
riodical, and my guess is that protecting the Shroud's reputation consists of nothing more than complete censorship

of anything that might cast doubt on the "authenticity" of the Shroud — even though the Catholic Church has never accepted it as an official relic.

As time passed, the members of the Centro began to think of themselves increasingly as more than just ex officio spiritual inheritors of the Shroud from the confraternity.

Since the Centro actually had no authority to grant permission to the American scientists or to anyone else to do any research on the Shroud itself, Peter Rinaldi would have to approach the archbishop-cardinal of Turin and the king. However, because of the complex political interrelationships, Rinaldi thought that the Jumper-Jackson group should present its experimental designs to the Centro.

The small American team went to Turin, where they were met by Fathers Rinaldi and Otterbein and escorted to a building and into a room dominated by a large table. There was a group of Italians, heavily loaded with clerics.

Jumper remembers: "We were ill at ease, and the Italians seemed very suspicious and chilly toward us. But we had brought with us a bunch of the *Proceedings* volumes, and we passed them out. You could see that they were impressed. I don't know how many could read English, but with the illustrations and equations and all, we made an impact."

John Jackson began talking, with Father Rinaldi acting as translator, and the meeting went on for hours. "At some point, the entire tone seemed to change. I can't pinpoint it, but the Italians began to act differently. I am sure it was those *Proceedings*."

Jackson had not been made aware of the fact that the Centro had no authority in the matter. He and his fellow team members made as convincing a case as they possibly could and returned home to await the verdict.

After they returned to the United States, they were in somewhat of a holding pattern till word came.

Of course, this did not apply to the irrepressible Jackson. His mind never stops. He recalled hearing somewhere that many modern machine tools, such as automated lathes, which turn out complex parts, are controlled by computer. He sought out Jumper.

"Eric, think about computer-controlled machine tools. Since the Shroud is a 3-D image ascertained by a computer in the VP-8, why can't we get data from the computer and feed them into a machine tool and turn out a statue of the man on the Shroud?"

Jumper thought about it and replied, "It should be possible. But first we have to get computer-generated contour curves."

That seemed reasonable, and they proceeded to try it. It did not work, because of a variety of complicated electrical and electronic reasons having to do with circuitry. This was frustrating, since it was obvious that it should work. Rudy Dichtl was not available, so they recruited John (Dee) German, whose background was very similar to Rudy's.

German plunged into the electronic guts of the computer and made some changes. Then he added some more instrumentation and fiddled and diddled until he was satisfied. Jackson and Jumper again tried making contour curves from horizontal scans across the body every few millimeters, and finally obtained the curves they sought.

Now that they had the data to feed into a computer-controlled machine tool, presto! out should come a statue. They decided to go to Denver, where, they thought, some top-flight aerospace companies certainly would have the latest and the best in such devices.

They found a group of engineers who were, at first, most eager to be helpful. But when Jumper and Jackson explained what they needed, and demonstrated the curves and mathematics, the chief engineer's jaw dropped. He shook his head helplessly and told the scientists that the best machine-tool computer rigs were about four light years behind what was required. There was not a prayer that any existing or planned instrumentation could cope with their problem.

Both men were discouraged. It is extremely annoying to know that something is perfectly feasible, only to find that the hardware to do it is nonexistent. On the drive from Denver back to Colorado Springs they discussed it.

"John, it makes me angry that we have a really simple problem, but there's no device powerful enough to do it."

That hit a nerve in Jackson, and he replied, "Power. That's all we need — power. And, by gosh, we have it."

"We do?"

"Sure. Cadet power. All we have to do is ask some cadets at the academy to volunteer in their spare time. We can generate computer curves, and have cadets cut each curve out of cardboard. Then we'll just pile the pieces of cardboard on top of each other, and we'll have a cardboard statue."

Jumper mulled it over. "You're right. Congratulations. You have just proved that a theoretician can join the real world every once in a while."

They readily obtained all the volunteers they could use. Jackson set up a schedule, and Jumper cleared out his garage for them to work in. They procured a huge amount of cardboard, along with shears and glue, curves and cadets. Work began on the basis of a twelve-to-sixteen-hour day. The pile grew and grew, until the last piece was in place. Jackson was extremely proud of it, but when his wife took a look, her comment was dismaying: "It looks all wrong. It's too flat."

Jackson realized that they had forgotten to subtract the Shroud-body distance. The life-size statue had the contours *of the cloth covering a body,* not of *the body itself.* If they subtracted the cloth-body distance factor, they should be able to see what the man himself looked like.

They made a new set of curves. Cadet power was again called on; a new statue rose in cardboard. When it was finished, Jackson's wife came to inspect it. "That's more like it," she said. The same statue, crafted in fiber glass, now stands in the Air Force Academy chapel.

One day early in 1978, Father Rinaldi phoned Jackson and told him there was a qualified green light. Enormous excitement rippled through the whole gaggle of Americans. Preparations were stepped up. More scientists were taken on board. One of them was Thomas D'Muhala, a nuclear physicist.

Tom is a great bear of a man. Large in stature and girth, fully bearded, he looks as though he may be ferocious. Instead, he is gentle and kindly and owns and runs a very complex and successful firm — Nuclear Technology, in Amston, Connecticut — whose primary function is to step in when nuclear reactors go wonky, from minor problems to a Three Mile Island–type of aberration. D'Muhala, by his own testimony, was a theological zero. "As far as I was concerned," he said, "science was my God."

D'Muhala had happened across a news story in a technical journal which mentioned that the Shroud was being investigated by scientists, including some from Los Alamos and others from the Air Force Academy. His curiosity piqued by this — because it sounded so odd — D'Muhala decided to call Los Alamos. He had spent quite a bit of time there and knew some of the scientists well. He gave the article to his secretary, and asked her to put in a call to one of the men at Los Alamos. By mistake, she put in the call to John Jackson at the Air Force Academy. Had D'Muhala spoken to anyone at Los Alamos, no one knows what would have ensued. But he found himself talking to the Pied Piper, and his involvement was virtually assured. Jackson invited D'Muhala to attend the next meeting of the team, to be held in May at Colorado Springs. D'Muhala accepted. However, he was on the verge of canceling several times. He was called to Japan, and would miss the meeting. The Japanese business terminated early, so he thought he could make Colorado Springs on the return voyage. Aboard his plane, a passenger died and the plane was diverted to Anchorage, Alaska. He would miss his connections and would have to cancel. By a fluke, an extra plane was added late to part of the route, and he felt he might make it. This aircraft was diverted by weather to Denver and was the last plane to land before the airport was socked in, with nothing leaving. Surely, this was the end of the enterprise, he felt. Then he stumbled across a stranger in the airport who decided to drive to Colorado Springs. Would D'Muhala like to come with him? It was on again. After becoming lost in the Rockies and losing his luggage, he still somehow made the meeting.

The May meeting turned out to be a high-pressure gathering for several disparate reasons. If the scientists got permission, as seemed likely, to go to Turin and examine the Shroud, there was (a) no money, (b) no equipment, (c) no idea of how many hours of hands-on time would be available, and (d) no idea what to do about a, b, and c. None of the research proposals had as yet been turned into concrete protocols, and there is a sizable difference between saying one would like to do X-ray fluorescence studies because they can show elemental composition, and constructing a definitive protocol. Most protocols are first drawn up as research proposals to obtain grants, and it may take from six to nine months to write one. It was now May, and everything had to be ready to go by September. Everyone on the team was a working scientist. There was not an administrator, fund raiser, coordinator, or expedition leader in the group. They were not even aware they needed any.

As always happens in such a situation, you go with your strength, which was science. Every scientist can put together a protocol and research plan, and that is what the team focused on. It really was all rather silly, because without the equipment, experiments cannot happen. Further, how can you write research plans when you have no idea of how much time there will be to carry out the investigation — minutes, hours, days? And, finally, obtaining the equipment, arranging for logistical back-up, and shipping everything, including all the scientists (now approaching thirty) to Turin, plus paying for room and board, all requires lots and lots of money. Nonetheless, the scientists spent their precious hours at the task they knew best, planning experiments.

While everyone was outlining the protocols he would write up, D'Muhala sat silently by in wonderment. Everyone was planning in a fiscal, temporal, and logistic vacuum. Finally, he raised his hand. Jackson recognized him, and D'Muhala stood up, a stranger to all except Jackson, who knew him only by phone.

"It seems to me," he said softly, "that you'll need some kind of versatile support system on which to place and hold the Shroud while all these experiments are going forward. If you wish, I'll be happy to build such a system. I'll just need its parameters.

"Next, I suspect that you'll require some money and equipment. I will try to provide them, if this is acceptable.

"Also, it seems obvious to me that there may be some severe organizational and logistical problems. If you desire, I will provide answers to both."

Had I been a member of the team at that time, I would have thought D'Muhala was either a bit potty or a rich eccentric. I would have been wrong on both counts, and luckily the Shroud team had no such reservations. Someone had just offered salvation, and who were they to quibble. From that minute on, whenever anyone had a nonscientific problem, it evoked a single response: "Let Tom take care of it." No one knew D'Muhala, his company, his track record, ability, or competence. As a matter of fact, Tom himself did not know whether he could pull off this set of miracles by September — just a shade over three months away.

In my thirty-five years of raising money for science, I have found that it takes a minimum of twelve months from an initial contact to the receipt of a check. A 5–10 percent success rate for each hundred applications is good. And D'Muhala had never raised any money for an eleemosynary purpose before. He was proposing to take on a gargantuan task.

On the evening of the first day of the conference, four

men sat down to design a table to hold the Shroud. It would be made of aluminum, but the flat top would have steel slats so that one or more slats could be removed, and the Shroud could be examined from the back. A duplicate set of slats was to be made of aluminum. The table top would rotate so that it could stand vertically. Large bar magnets coated with Teflon would be built to hold the cloth gently but firmly to the surface in a horizontal and vertical mode. According to the JPL men, drawing up such a complex design would take about six weeks in their shop. Here it was done in three hours.

Jackson called Father Otterbein to see if he could obtain for them an idea of just how long the hands-on period would be. The priest told him that they might not know until they arrived in Turin. Jackson reported this to Jumper, who thought about it for a moment, and said: "All right. We'll have to have everyone put his experiments in a rigorous time frame — preferably blocks. Then, when we have everyone's protocol, we can plan on the basis of twelve hours, or twenty-four, thirty-six, forty-eight, seventy-two, ninety-six, and assign priorities."

This element of time constraint is alien to most basic-research investigations. To take just one example, X-ray fluorescence requires that each area to be measured will be examined for about four hours. The assumption is that there is an amount of material being measured well above the threshold detection level, and that there will be enough data points to be statistically significant. Every investigator tries to obtain the best possible statistics in any experiment. If he is forced to reduce the time, he will be able to detect less and be less sure of his results because of statistical spread. In this experiment, restrictions on time would mean that fewer areas on the Shroud could be sampled. To meet any contingency, everyone was sent off with firm orders to design protocols complete with timetables and time constraints in blocks.

Three days after the meeting ended, Father Otterbein

called Jumper to tell him that he had just received word that the scientists had been scrubbed. Jumper made a fast, command decision: he would not tell the team. If he turned them off, they would probably stay off, even if the decision was reversed. And somehow, he felt, it just had to be reversed. He discussed it with Jackson, who agreed.

It was a fortunate decision, for ten days later Father Rinaldi called and told them the light was green again. No momentum had been lost.

· 4 ·

An Odd and Wondrous Way
to Organize an Expedition

TOM D'MUHALA returned home to Connecticut, wondering what sort of lunacy had got him involved in the Shroud project. He sat at his desk and thought about how he was going to squeeze everything into his schedule.

Then he sent for his corporate treasurer and friend, George Markoski. As D'Muhala described his commitment to his finance man, Markoski saw profits vanishing while the chief executive officer rode off on a project of knight-errantry. Markoski has only two modes of conduct: he either hates you or loves you. It has nothing to do with the individual's personality, but with what he has just done. Thus, Markoski can hate and love the same person three times a day. He never hates very long, but when he does, he is both loud and colorful. D'Muhala knows how to act in these situations. He just goes about his business while George vents his spleen and finally cools down.

Markoski told D'Muhala, "You realize that this is the stupidest thing you have ever done? The business can't afford your taking off all the time this will require. Are you out of your mind?"

Tom just nodded.

After Markoski got everything off his chest, he added, as is his style, "O.K. Now what can I do to help?"

In that moment Markoski became treasurer of the Shroud project.

D'Muhala told Markoski that the scientists were a large, disorganized covey. There was no official leader; everything was done on an ad hoc basis; there was no general communication mechanism, no chain of command — nothing. He decided that there had to be a minimal structure and organization. The two of them set out to create a corporation to give the project a measure of organization. They established a nonstock, nonprofit, Connecticut-based corporation to be run for and by the participating scientists, solely for the limited purpose of research on the Shroud. If the team was interested, D'Muhala would have the corporate structure ready for them to walk into.

Then came the problem of fund-raising. D'Muhala asked Markoski if he had any ideas.

"How much do we need?"

"Several hundreds of thousands of dollars, I guess."

Markoski went into orbit again. When he came down, he said, "The first thing we have to do is to try to get a tax-exempt status for the new corporation. If people can get a tax deduction, they may be more willing to give."

They asked their attorney to file with the IRS for a tax-exempt status. The attorney asked how soon they needed it.

The answer was "As soon as possible — at a maximum, three months."

The attorney shook his head. He pointed out that there was no way this could be done. It normally took no less than two years — *after* one had a year of successful work on whatever the project was about. D'Muhala instructed the lawyer to try anyway. He reluctantly agreed, but assured them that he knew of no case in which tax-exempt status was granted in less than a year after a previous year of successful activity. When the attorney asked for the corporation's name, D'Muhala and Markoski tried to think of one that would make a good acronym. Finally, they decided on "Shroud of Turin Research Project, Inc." — STURP, for short.

D'Muhala now tackled the manufacture of the table on which the Shroud would be placed for testing. Had it been ordered for commercial purposes, the cost would have been about $20,000 because of its complexity. He found a machinist who agreed to donate his labor to the effort.

Then D'Muhala returned to the problem of raising funds. Since he was a businessman, his first thought was to go to industrialists to see if they would contribute. Jackson and Jumper had provided him with a videotape of *The Silent Witness*. With this in hand, along with copies of the 1977 *Proceedings* at Albuquerque, he began making the rounds. Everywhere he went, he met with a courteous reception. Everyone seemed intrigued, but each time he was told that the particular corporation could not be perceived by the public and its stockholders as supporting a cause that might have religious significance in a secularist world. It would be bad for business. Although D'Muhala never turned down the $50 or $100 contributions they then offered, it did not take much arithmetic to figure that this would not do the trick. He began to try foundations. Here he ran once more into the secularist argument, and the fact that foundations take a long, long time to decide to award a grant — usually at least a year. That too was out. Clearly, the government would not contribute, for the same reason, and D'Muhala agreed with Jumper and Jackson that no church should be involved. That might be seen by the outside world as biasing any results the scientists obtained. This left only one possibility: donations by individuals of means. How could they be identified? And, after finding out who they are, how does one obtain access to them? Neither question is easy. The only course is to cover many miles, talk to many people, and keep asking questions.

D'Muhala went to friends, acquaintances, the governor of

Connecticut, the lieutenant governor, legislators, corporate executives; he even went up to Canada. Slowly, a trickle of money began to come in.

No one ever turned D'Muhala down. This is unheard of among people who seek grants. Refusals usually range from "Sorry, I gave at the office," to "I am not interested," or "My charitable budget is exhausted for this year." D'Muhala never once met with this.

But even as the money began to come in, the requests from team members for instrumentation, supplies, travel money, and similar costs began to mount. Markoski complained that he was just a circuit through which money ran. As fast as he received dollars from Tom, a team member would require them for a project, and out the funds would go. The need for money began to increase more rapidly than D'Muhala could raise it. At this point, members of the scientific team began to expend their own funds — money that would not be reimbursed. I know of none who did not put many hundreds or several thousands of dollars into the project; they sold vehicles or took out bank loans, or procured second mortgages and cleaned out savings accounts. This is not common knowledge even among the group, since it is not discussed, yet everyone wound up doing the same thing.

As knowledge spread through scientific circles that such a project was underway, team members were approached by various groups to give talks on the subject. They all complied, and they spoke at universities, scientific societies, churches, and fraternal organizations. It is customary for honorariums to be given to such speakers for their time and expertise. The payments are meant for them. In this singular endeavor, each investigator sent the funds to D'Muhala for the pot, though none was ever asked to do so. For totally diverse individuals — now about forty in number — to behave similarly in a fashion that is dissimilar to what they have done all their lives may be just another coincidence, but the funds were certainly piling up.

Soon D'Muhala began receiving requests from team members for big, expensive equipment. Some of the items cost in excess of $150,000. He decided that it was silly to beg for money and then buy instruments with it. Why not, he reasoned, go straight to the manufacturers and ask for the apparatus itself? Producers of scientific gear and supplies will often donate some of their product and then receive credit in the scientific papers that result. This is a low-key form of advertising. It could not be done in this instance, for Fathers Otterbein and Rinaldi had told team members that the Turinese authorities demanded complete confidentiality about the entire scientific endeavor. No one knew exactly who these authorities were, but it made sense, because the press had become alert to the possibility that American investigators might be permitted access to the Shroud. Scientists who had never spoken to any reporter were quoted as having said things that were patently absurd and arrant nonsense. This project was implicitly controversial, and completely irresponsible statements attributed to the team would make them sound like idiots.

D'Muhala was in the position of having to beg for equipment on a secret and confidential basis. Even so, by the end of the three-month period he had got, by gift and loan, close to $2.5 million worth of scientific apparatus. This is one of the most extraordinary virtuoso performances in my experience, but in this project, the improbable became commonplace, the impossible only slightly less frequent.

While he was begging for money and equipment and running Nuclear Technology, he also had to tackle immense logistical problems. First, he realized that the whole team must go through a dry run before heading for Europe. He decided to hold it on the long Labor Day weekend, in September, at his plant. After that weekend, all the hardware would be shipped to Italy. He would build shipping boxes and crates for everything — a job that called for painstaking work, for this type of instrumentation is fragile, and each piece has its own specific requirements. One of the most difficult was a detector that had to be kept in liquid nitrogen at −80°C. If the temperature ever rose above this point, the detector would be ruined, so it had to be shipped in a vacuum bottle, covered with liquid gas. The fluid could not be allowed to slosh, nor could it evaporate below a critical level. In order to keep the fluid at the proper level, additional liquid nitrogen had to be added from time to time. All these precautions were taken while the detector was shipped from Connecticut to Kennedy Airport, loaded on a plane and flown to Rome or Milan, off-loaded and trucked to Turin into customs, and finally trucked once more to the site. Anyone who has seen freight handlers and truckers sling crates will realize the problems involved.

Most complex devices could not be shipped intact. They had to be broken down into their component parts, which were then either packed by themselves or nested in separate structures within a larger container. Some instruments were constructed of components made by different manufacturers whose names and lot numbers were inscribed on the part. Each item was logged and catalogued for customs. All in all, the whole enterprise was time-consuming in the extreme. Before D'Muhala was through, he had over fifty volunteers, who obtained lumber, and packing materials, made measurements, designed and built crates, and numbered and labeled them. He also had to make sure that all shipping containers were reusable, for Italian customs demanded that each such item coming into the country was shipped back out.

D'Muhala realized that a dry run would not make much sense unless the scientists had something on which to perform their tests. He located a delightful octogenarian lady who made linen from flax and spun it by hand. Would she please make a fourteen-foot-long, three-and-a-half-foot-wide pseudo-Shroud out of linen in three months? Of course she would. D'Muhala contacted Vern Miller at the Brooks Institute, who found an artist to put life-size images of the front and back of a crucified man on the pseudo-Shroud in a color that matched the one in the photographs of the actual linen. Then the white linen would be steeped in tea until it had an ivory tone similar to the real Shroud.

Some of the apparatus was still being built — all the photographic gear, with fragile liquid filters, lights, ultraviolet and infrared sources — and would not be ready until just a couple of days before the team took off in early October. Not until just five days before takeoff would Vern Miller obtain a superb photomacroscope (a low-power microscope rigged for taking photographs). Working like a demon with volunteers, Miller broke it down and integrated it with the rest of his gear just in time.

D'Muhala then tackled the job of travel. The team was to assemble from all over the country at Nuclear Technology on Labor Day, work, return home, and, three and a half weeks after, gather in New York City to depart for Turin. He approached sixteen scheduled and nonscheduled airlines and began to haggle for the best price for team and cargo. This bargaining continued up to the final week.

During all this frenetic activity, Father Rinaldi was in his native Turin, acting as the Italian anchor man and as liaison with the cardinal, king, Turinese officialdom, the Centro di Sindonologia, clergy, customs, and the Italian government. His chore was particularly difficult, because over three million people were streaming into Turin to see the Shroud and to celebrate the four-hundredth anniversary of its arrival in that city. And at the end of the summer, just before the exhibition ended, there was to be a very large congress on the subject of the Sancta Sindone, the Holy Shroud. Father Rinaldi was heavily involved with all this activity.

He also had to make the hotel reservations for the scientists. One day in midsummer, Tom received a frantic telephone call from the priest. Because of the pilgrims coming to the city, the hotel had just announced that it would cancel the team's reservations unless it received an advance payment of $5000 within twenty-four hours. The hotel management was adamant. D'Muhala went to consult Markoski. The STURP bank account had only a few hundred dollars in it. Neither man had any liquid assets. Both had contributed what they could. They sat and stared at one another.

The men shared a hobby: they played the commodity market. D'Muhala called it a crap shoot, but both of them enjoyed the challenge of pitting their knowledge and guess-work against the market. Together, they had $3200 invested. While they were wondering how to pay the advance, the phone rang. It was their broker.

"You guys are really lucky. There was a spurt in the market. We had a batch of stop-sell orders, including yours. Right after the rise, prices dropped like a stone, and yours was the only stop-sell order that was executed. You now have five thousand dollars between you. Do you want to reinvest?"

A big smile covered Markoski's face. He looked at D'Muhala, who nodded.

"No," he said, "we'll take it out."

A $5000 money order was wired to the hotel that afternoon.

Early in August, while the procuring of instruments, the building of crates, and the rest of the logistics were underway, D'Muhala and Markoski had to consult their attorneys on a business problem. As they entered his office, he asked them, "Do you fellows have strings that you pull in the Internal Revenue Service?"

"No," said D'Muhala. "Why?"

"Then it has to be some kind of bureaucratic miracle. The tax-exempt status for STURP came through. You got it in just a couple of months. It's ridiculous!"

D'Muhala just smiled and nodded. Within a short period, he was becoming used to the improbable. The impossible was merely evoking a smile.

Next on D'Muhala's list was the problem of electrical power and water for the equipment in Turin, and its maintenance and repair. All of the team's apparatus required 120-

volt, 60-cycle electricity. In Italy, the power is delivered at 240 volts, 50 cycles. Furthermore, scientists never have enough watts to work with — ever. At this juncture, two vital men re-entered the scene — Rudy Dichtl and Dee German.

Both were physicists, and they agreed to take care of the utilities. "Leave it to us," they said. "If each team member gives us a schematic [electrical wiring diagram] and, where possible, a manual, we'll bring along spares of parts that are likely to go. If anything else conks out, we'll knock something together." Neither Dichtl nor German had a project of his own, so they undertook to support everyone else's.

Having accepted Jackson's invitation to the Amston meeting, I was reading up on the historical background of the Shroud. No one seems to know where Geoffrey de Charny obtained it. Of course, if it wasn't forged, it had to have come from somewhere — and that problem opened up a whole new can of squirming worms.

Clearly, if it came from the West, it was a forgery. If it did not originate in the West, then it must have come from the East — where it may also have been forged. If it came from the East, how did it get to the West? The overwhelming probability is that it was acquired during one of the crusades. And, of the crusades, the most likely is the fourth. A lowly French knight named Robert de Clari claimed he had seen the Shroud.

Is there any evidence that this occurred? The answer is yes — perhaps. When Constantine gained control of the entire Roman Empire and converted to Christianity, he established his rule in Byzantium, in the East, and in A.D. 330 renamed the capital city Byzantium, after himself — Constantinople. His empire was the bastion of Christendom, and the affluence and culture of Constantinople became legendary. The Byzantine Empire was probably the only one where religious questions and beliefs became the basis for political parties, and where politics and theology were so entwined that they were one.

The Fourth Crusade set out, as had the others, to free the Holy Land from the infidel. The army was composed primarily of French and Venetians, the latter being led by a crafty doge, Enrico Dandolo. Dandolo was close to ninety years old and blind, a man of remarkable energy, with vast experience in politics and commerce. His primary function was to make sure that the mercantile interests of Venice prospered — even if he had to conquer Christian lands to achieve this.

The French allied forces on the Fourth Crusade were led by counts, barons, and a marquis, none of them a match for Dandolo. As rich and powerful as was Venice, it had rivals, which included Zara, on the Adriatic Sea, and Byzantium, both of them Christian. The crusaders never reached the Holy Land. Instead, under the influence of the doge, they laid siege to and captured Zara and Constantinople. The crusaders sacked, looted, and raped. Though some historians feel that all this was the result of a series of accidents, others believe that it was because of Dandolo's cupidity. The sack of both cities rid Venice of two rivals, and "the Queen of the Adriatic" took much plunder, some of which, such as the great bronze horses above the portico of the Basilica of San Marco, can be seen in Venice today.

There are several primary sources of the history of the Fourth Crusade written by participants — one of them, Robert de Clari. Robert came from Picardy, and when he entered Constantinople he was so bedazzled by its splendor and wealth that his narrative has all the breathless sense of wonder, surprise, and awe of a country boy who has visited the capital of the world — which, in effect, Constantinople was. In Robert's narrative, he states that he visited the Church of Our Lady of Blachernae, "where was kept the shroud in which Our Lord had been wrapped, which [was] stood up straight every Friday so that the figure of

Our Lord could be plainly seen there — and, no one, either Greek [Byzantine] or French, ever knew what became of this shroud after the city was taken."

One of the reasons I like science is that there is usually a way to obtain an answer and test it. History, on the contrary, is much more slippery. To check on the Byzantine origins of the Shroud, I went to Dumbarton Oaks to hear a lecture by a visiting professor of ancient history on the history of the Shroud and St. Veronica's Veil. The two pieces of cloth are now inextricably interwoven because Ian Wilson thought of an intriguing link between them. Carelessness and confusion on the part of translators and some clerics has led many to believe that there is a connection between the two items. But as far as I can tell, there is none whatsoever. It takes some dissection to reach this conclusion — or, in scientific parlance, to extract the signal from the noise.

St. Veronica's Veil is confusing because there was no Veronica per se in the first century. The name is a compound of Latin and Greek words: *vera*, meaning truth; *icon*, meaning a picture or representation. There was indeed a picture of Christ's head, which dates back to about the fifth century. It is occasionally called the Abgar or Edessa image. However, most scholars — Byzantine and Western — are agreed that it was a completely apocryphal picture, as were the stories behind it. At one time, the Arabs captured it and reputedly made at least one copy; later, many other copies were made. Hence the search for the *vera icon*. Whoever decided which one was the "true picture," it wound up in the emperor's trove of relics and disappeared after the Fourth Crusade, along with everything else. Ian Wilson presented the hypothesis that the vera icon — also called the Mandylion (derived from the Arabic) — was really the Shroud of Turin, with all fourteen feet folded so that only the face showed. I have spoken to no serious historian who gives credence to this essentially fictional story. While the visiting professor was taking apart the Wilson hypothesis, she mentioned Robert de Clari. Up to that point, I had been taking Robert at face value. The statement was made that Robert had not only identified the Shroud in the Church of Our Lady of Blachernae, but also in the Pharos Chapel, which was clear across the city of Constantinople. Obviously, he could not be taken seriously. I didn't recall this contradiction, and decided to read Robert's account again. I found the passage about Blachernae. I could not find a mention of a Shroud at Pharos. But there was something a lot worse. The latest English translation was done in 1936 by E. H. McNeal. In the key passage about the Shroud, McNeal does not translate the word "shroud" into English, but for some reason leaves it in medieval French, *sydoine*. That was all right, but then he added a footnote that really put the fox in the hen house: "Robert seems to have confused *sudarium* (the sweat cloth or napkin, the True Image of St. Veronica) with the *sindon* (the grave cloth in which the body of Jesus was wrapped for entombment). Both relics were in the church of the Blessed Virgin in the Great Palace (Pharos), and not in the church in the palace of Blachernae, as Robert says."

Here I was, an ordinary run-of-the-mill scientist trying to establish a few reference points in my mind about this thing with which I might become involved, and I found that instead of enlightenment from the historians, I got nothing but static.

Looking at McNeal's footnote again, I shook my head and went back to the original French. After wrestling with it for a while, I decided to consult another translation of Robert. This more modern one, in Italian, was by A. N. Padrone. She concurs that Robert was wrong to identify the Shroud in Blachernae, but her reasoning is nonexistent — she was probably just following McNeal, who also gives no reason.

I was extremely skeptical that seven hundred years after the event, McNeal could say that an eyewitness:

1. Did not know what he saw and/or misnamed it, or
2. Did not know where he was and/or misnamed the place, or
3. Both.

The only medieval French synonym for sydoine, as far as I know, is *suaire.* The *sudarium* (sweat cloth, vera icon, Mandylion, napkin, or what have you) was, by all accounts and pictures back to A.D. 945, very small. One would not have to "stand it up straight" or "be stood up straight" to see the "face," as McNeal translates it. Robert uses the word "figure." "Face" is a modern translation of "figure." The medieval word "figure" meant figure, form, appearance. Besides which, Robert was undoubtedly illiterate and dictated his memoirs to a scribe. The original document has vanished. A copy, or a copy of a copy, was made in about 1300, and wound up in Copenhagen, where, in 1873, a German published it. It contained numerous errors. In 1924, in a series of medieval French classics, the French scholar M. P. Lauer also published a version. When I reached for Lauer, I felt more comfortable: I would rather rely on a French medievalist. He translates Robert with no hesitation or footnote about the sydoine being in Blachernae. I even found the historical reference that McNeal thought gave him the right to say Robert was wrong. McNeal had misread it.

After all the historical *Sturm und Drang,* I was glad to return to science. At least I had found one historical eyewitness who described something that might reasonably have been the Shroud in the East around 1200. Later, I would find another from the preceding century.

There were other references I found in the dark and distant past that had been mentioned on occasion by scholars. But after I had unearthed them from some dusty library stacks, I decided they were too vague for me to take seriously. There was one exception. It was a catalogue put together by an Icelandic abbot named Nicholas Soemundarson, who in 1157 returned home after a pilgrimage to Constantinople. I was spellbound at the thought of the transportation problem. The only means available to him for such a trip was a Viking-type vessel with one sail and oars. In the likely event he went by sea, the whole trip was about 3400 miles each way! When I was through fantasizing about such a voyage, I turned my attention to the list of relics that the abbot had drawn up. Again, I decided I could not rely on a translation and sought out the original. To my horror, it was not in Latin but medieval Icelandic. A dictionary of that exotic language is not to be found at one's friendly local library. Finally, with the good offices of Yale's associate librarian, Donald Engley, I found what I needed. I will accept the abbot's mention of a "shroud with the blood and body of Christ on it" as evidence that Robert de Clari saw what he claimed. If there is an earlier reference, I have yet to find it.

· 5 ·

Preparation and Protocols:
The Dry Run

IN MID-AUGUST 1978, I received in the mail a Xerographic copy of an announcement of the meeting in Amston. I have received hundreds of similar announcements; they are usually printed, or at least photo-offset. This one was badly typed on an antique typewriter and filled with misspellings and sentence fragments. It emphasized that coffee and doughnuts would be available every two hours, and stressed that *they*, but nothing else, would be free. A few of the details it contained were downright wild. There would be a "clean blackboard with a clean eraser, and a new piece of chalk plus ash trays." Regarding eating arrangements: "Candles on tables, no cocktails required." At best, it was droll. At worst, it looked like the attempt of seventh-grade youngsters to write science fiction. I had never heard of Amston before Jackson mentioned it to me on the phone a few weeks earlier. As a lifelong resident of Connecticut, I thought I knew of every village in the state. Finally, I located it as a pinprick on my most definitive map. Whoever heard of a scientific colloquium in the boondocks over Labor Day, featuring a new piece of chalk? My earlier reservations about having anything to do with this project flared up once more.

I brooded about it. My curiosity is a constant, but my fears are not, and they fluttered thickly about me like bats in the night. I decided I would not have anything further to do with the project, and would let the whole thing drop. Besides, there was going to be a big family get-together over Labor Day — all seven children and grandchildren. File and forget the Shroud.

Three days before the long weekend, because of a series of odd coincidences, the family affair evaporated; everyone had opted to attend some competing activity. Since a long empty weekend loomed, I thought I might as well go up to Amston and peek in on the project, for it was only a couple of hours' drive. Just in case my apprehensions were unjustified, I packed a bag.

The Sheraton Motor Inn in Norwich was the sleeping headquarters for the conferees, and the first item on the agenda was breakfast.

By the time I arrived, I had psyched myself into a distinctly negative frame of mind. So much so that when I parked the car I purposely left my suitcase in it. I was reasonably sure that this was not going to be my cup of tea.

I entered and proceeded to the dining room for breakfast. I sat down alone, although I saw other men who, judging by the occasional word I could overhear, were obviously scientists. As I watched them and sipped coffee, I noted that their conversations were extremely intense.

Then a black man entered the dining room, and the others rose and embraced him in a huge hug. More men entered, and the performance was repeated.

It struck me as bizarre. I had never seen anything like this among scientific professionals. A smile, a greeting, a handshake — but everyone embracing one another? It was eccentric, to say the least. These people were extravagantly pleased to see one another.

Then three Catholic priests entered and were similarly greeted.

"That does it," I groaned to myself. "It's a Catholic show.

It will be biased as hell, and that's scientific anathema."

But as I rose to leave, the entire group did too, effectively surrounding me and bearing me along to a conference room.

"Well," I thought, "I guess it won't hurt just to stick around for an hour. Just don't forget, you're only going to *test* the water."

At the room's entrance, names were asked and two lists were checked. The security measures reminded me of a visit I'd once paid to the director of the CIA.

Inside the room, everyone sat at one huge table. I looked around and suddenly recognized a face. The man was a director of the imaging team for the NASA Viking project. Then I recognized another. I felt better at once — *they* were certainly not amateurs.

John Jackson, the leader of the team, rose and called the meeting to order.

"Our first priority," he said, "is security. In order to have the opportunity to work with the Shroud itself, we've had to promise the authorities in Turin to keep every aspect of our work secret. Is there anyone here who has never worked on a project involving security — secret, top secret?"

Not a single hand was raised. Obviously, this was not a bunch of amateurs.

"Good," declared Jackson. "The biggest problem we have is the press. They're all over this hotel. They're incredible. Go to a restaurant where you didn't plan to go, and they're there within thirty minutes. I don't know how they do it, but they're everywhere, and they use hidden microphones, as well as obvious ones. So don't talk to anyone who isn't on the team. As a matter of fact, we're not even supposed to acknowledge that we've been given permission to do the testing or that we're going to Turin."

That the group actually had permission to go to Italy and do hands-on work with the Shroud was exciting news to me. But for an expedition of several dozen people to go to Turin incognito without the media finding out was, I thought, going to be a neat trick.

Jackson turned the floor over to Eric Jumper, who explained that no one knew how much time the team would actually have to spend with the Shroud. They would have to make contingency plans, and the experiments must be set up in order of priority.

The lights were dimmed, and a projector flashed on a screen. On it was a photo of the pseudo-Shroud D'Muhala had had made, and superimposed on it was a grid.

Jumper said, "You'll each be given a sheet with this grid. We have protocols of most of the experiments, and the rest must be in by the end of this weekend."

He flashed on the screen the list of experiments that would be performed if only twelve hours were allotted, with the names of the team members and the equipment to be used. This was followed by the twenty-four-hour protocol, the thirty-six, forty-eight, and the sixty-hour plans — each with the experiments, investigators, gear, and timing.

The proposal was extremely well thought out and meticulously planned. I was impressed. This was science with a capital S. It was equally obvious that no one had an a priori bias about the Shroud's provenance. Most of the experiments were designed to determine whether it was a forgery or the result of body chemistry. Other physical and chemical possibilities were not excluded, and every type of nondestructive test for which the equipment could be transported to Turin was included. This gear would produce reams of data that should cover all eventualities.

Jumper finished his talk, and Jackson continued the presentation.

"Tom D'Muhala has, for good and sufficient reason, created a corporate entity in the state of Connecticut. It is a nonstock, nonprofit, tax-exempt corporation, and all of us are the corporation. It will be called the Shroud of Turin Research Project, Inc., or STURP. The major purpose of STURP is to ensure the integrity of this project. No church, no religious group, no group of any kind, will or can influence STURP."

"Hallelujah!" I thought.

Jackson continued: "STURP will be a free-standing entity, and donors can obtain an exemption for any funds contributed. Furthermore, to make the decision of the board of trustees binding on the membership, and to secure the secrecy requested by Turin, I am asking you all to sign the agreement that's being passed around."

Sheets of paper were circulated, and as the scientists scanned them, one or two shook their heads. Someone muttered, "No way am I going to sign this."

Jackson asked what the problem was. As some investigators saw it, the secrecy posed a possible threat to their freedom to publish in scientific journals.

"Suppose," asked Joseph Accetta, the infrared expert on the team, "the authorities in Turin decide that the secrecy should be permanent? They could prevent us from ever publishing our results freely in scientific journals. They could also use this secrecy clause as a form of censorship if they don't like the results of our work."

It was a good point. A member of the X-ray fluorescence team stated emphatically that if he were not free to publish whatever he found, he wouldn't go to Turin.

After some discussion, modifications which precluded that possibility were agreed to. Then everyone signed. In doing so, I became a member of STURP.

There followed more talks, one by Father Peter Rinaldi, who had just returned from Italy. He sketched in the politics of Shroud research. The clerical head of the Centro di Sindonologia was Don Coero. The key figure there was the science adviser, a physician who held a post equivalent to medical examiner of Turin — Dr. Pierluigi Baima Bollone. The Centro hoped that Baima would be science director for any observations that might be made. There was also the Communist mayor of Turin, who felt that the Shroud belonged to the city. Then there was the priest of the chapel in which the Shroud was kept, as well as the canon and custodian of the Shroud. Finally, there was

Archbishop-Cardinal Balestrero, who had, along with the king, ultimate authority over the Shroud.

As Father Rinaldi was spinning his intricate analysis, I thought, "Wheels within wheels within wheels. Sensibilities will have to be watched very carefully."

Father Rinaldi was followed by D'Muhala, who discussed the logistical details. He told us that the trial run would follow this gathering. All of the equipment was in open crates. It would be taken out, tested, and then replaced, ready to go. We would spend the next two days choreographing who would do what, in what sequence, and how. It would be a full-scale attempt to debug the scientific procedures prior to Turin.

Then there came the famous coffee and doughnuts. I was sufficiently pleased by what I had heard so far to go to the parking lot, bring in my valise, and check into a room at the inn.

Following the break, the meeting came to order once more, and two men rose to speak. One was Ernie Brooks; and the other, Vern Miller. Both had just come back from Turin, where they had gone in advance of the team in order to make a preliminary appraisal of the optical characteristics of the Shroud. Most of the tests the team was to perform were in the realm of physics, which required "looking" at the cloth. As much forehand knowledge as possible would help the scientists to calibrate their instruments accordingly.

In Turin, Brooks and Miller had visited the Cathedral of St. John, where the Shroud was displayed high above the altar in a bulletproof-glass-covered container filled with inert gas.

Miller was a Mormon; Brooks, a Presbyterian. Neither had ever been in a Catholic cathedral before. Brooks began to describe his experience in watching his first High Mass.

"I have never witnessed such pageantry. The acoustics were powerful in this ancient cathedral; there was candlelight, ringing of bells, and a choir. There must have been two thousand people packed in there. Finally, they all left, and we wanted to take photographic close-ups. With the help of Father Rinaldi and another priest, we got a ten-foot ladder, but it barely reached the top of the altar. So we put the ladder on antique coin boxes, and Vern and I started to climb up, trying to avoid knocking over sixteenth-century icons. But Vern had room for only one leg, so he put the other on my shoulder. Father Rinaldi was trying to keep that leg from slipping off."

Miller continued, "I broke out my tripod, but there was room for only two of its legs. So the priests ran around collecting antique stands, furnishings, and so forth, and built a stand for my third tripod leg."

Suddenly, Brooks, who was balancing Miller on one shoulder, looked up and said, "Jesus Christ, Vern, I think the blood on the face is crimson." His voice echoed through the cathedral.

Miller hissed, "Ernie, watch your language"; then, in a more normal voice, added, "Well, at least you called Him by the right name."

After getting the photographs and the light readings, the two men went back to the hotel to pack. While waiting for the bus, Vern engaged in conversation with a reporter from Switzerland. Miller had seen some spots on the Shroud, which later turned out to be candle wax. He mentioned them to the reporter, saying they were almost the color of chicken soup. By the time they reached the airport for their flight to New York, the latest edition of a Geneva newspaper was on the stands, with the headline "Shroud Scientist Finds Chicken Soup." No one had to emphasize to Miller and Brooks not to chat with the media. Both men had come directly from Turin to brief the team.

At the next break, I went up to Jackson and introduced myself. He looked at me with a blank face.

"Holy crow," I thought, "he doesn't even remember who I am."

Before I could refresh Jackson's memory, the leader of STURP was engulfed by a swarm of team members. Disconcerted by my reception, I sought out Ray Rogers and introduced myself to him. A lean Westerner with a ready smile and a friendly and gracious manner, Rogers said he was looking forward to working with me. But before any more could be said, he too was dragged off by another group of team members. An announcement was made that the team would board a bus to go to D'Muhala's plant. As we left the room, the reporters, armed with microphones and videocameras, swooped down on us and, like cowboys cutting particular steers from a herd, separated and cornered individual scientists.

The team members, some with seriocomic faces, others with clenched jaws, muttered inconsequential inanities and struggled their way through the lobby, out the front door, and into the bus heading to Nuclear Technology. The reporters followed in pursuit all the way to the plant, where they found themselves turned away at the door, with one exception. A team from the *National Geographic*, headed up by Ken Weaver, who had previously agreed to abide by all the rules and secrecy that STURP required, were welcomed as representatives of the most responsible, accurate, and dispassionate of popular journals.

As the team filed into a huge room lined with black plastic and lit with klieg lights, it beheld a dramatic diorama. All around the sides of the room were open packing crates filled with the sophisticated scientific equipment needed for Turin. In the center of the room was the large, specially made steel table, and on it was a fourteen-foot-long, three-and-a-half-foot-wide linen cloth — the simulacrum of the Shroud — with life-size pictures of the front and back of a crucified man.

The team stood there for a moment, mesmerized.

Jackson thought to himself, "Gosh, we're really going to do it."

Don Devan, the computer and image-enhancement scientist, said to himself, "Hey! Not bad. This really looks like science."

I weighed the spectacle and mused, "Well, this really is a serious effort. Those life-size images somehow look larger than life."

Eric Jumper thought, "Great, we're in business."

Then, almost as if by signal, the thirty-six members of the scientific team began to assemble, test, and rig the equipment. There was also about a score of assistants, facilitators, and trouble-shooters. Everyone converged around the seventeen-foot-long, four-foot-wide table. Such a mass of researchers in so small an area presaged chaos.

The minimum laboratory working space in terms of available lab bench is five linear feet per person — in the most crowded university situation. This averages out to about fifteen square feet per researcher. Here, there were thirty-six primary investigators, most of whom had never worked together before, plus assistants, crowding around a table whose total area was sixty-eight square feet. The absolute minimum space for any kind of effective working environment for thirty-six individual scientists, plus twenty assistants, should be 840 square feet. Now, each individual was crowded into about one twentieth of the area of the minimum laboratory situation. In addition, many different experiments requiring different investigators and devices were planned for the same areas, for example, the presumed lance wound on the side. Further, many of these experiments were physically incompatible. For one set of investigations, bright white light would be needed; for others, such as infrared studies, pitch-blackness would be required. Some investigators would be using X rays, which would be hazardous to all other workers. Others needed intense ultraviolet light, which could destroy unshielded eyes. A few instruments produced significant vibration, which was intolerable for other work. Such a stew, with so many people who were really still strangers to one another in fact as well as in a

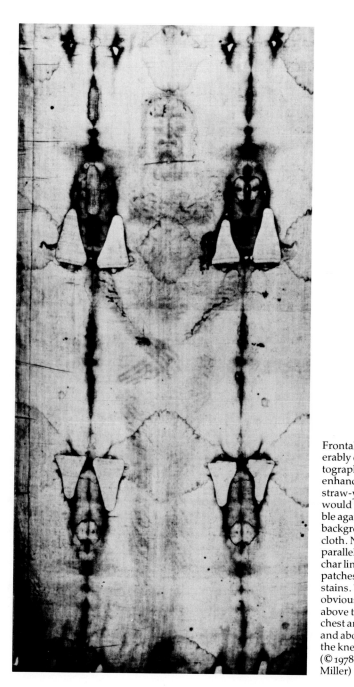

Frontal image considerably enhanced photographically. Without enhancement, the straw-yellow image would be almost invisible against the ivory background of the cloth. Note the two parallel scorch-and-char lines, the eight patches, and the water stains. The three most obvious stains are above the head, at mid-chest and abdomen, and above and below the knees.
(© 1978 by Vernon D. Miller)

Left: $2.5 million worth of scientific equipment finally arrives at the royal palace in Turin after a nearly disastrous delay. (© 1978 by Barrie M. Schwortz)

Below: John Jackson chairs one of the many brainstorming sessions in the ornate Shroud test room. (© 1978 by Ernest H. Brooks II)

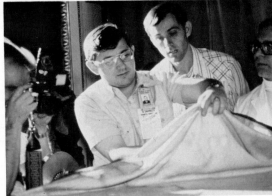

Left: The Shroud is placed on the test table by members of the American scientific team. (© 1978 by Ernest H. Brooks II)

Above: Scientists examine the underside of the Shroud. Left to right: Miller (with camera), Jumper, Jackson, and Riggi. (© 1978 by Ernest H. Brooks II)

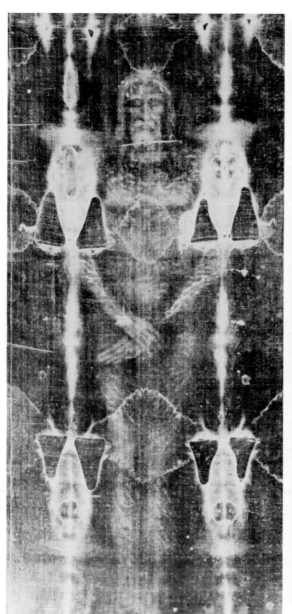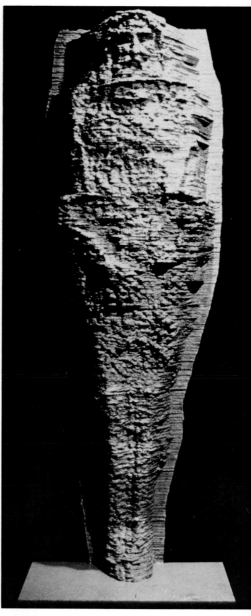

On the left, the frontal image, enhanced photographically, is seen as a positive on this film negative. On the right, a cardboard statue, constructed according to electronic translations of the VP-8 image of the Shroud. Note that owing to the VP-8 all darker features—such as the water stains and blood—appear to be in raised relief. (© 1978 by Vernon D. Miller)

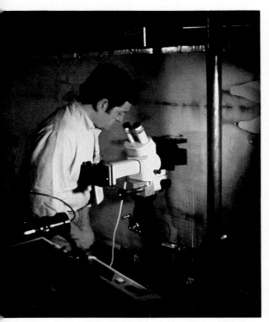

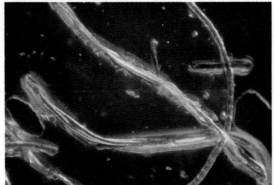

Above: Don Devan examining the Shroud through a macroscope. (© 1978 by Vernon D. Miller)

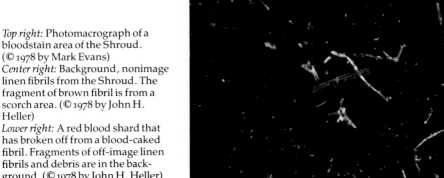

Top right: Photomacrograph of a bloodstain area of the Shroud. (© 1978 by Mark Evans)
Center right: Background, nonimage linen fibrils from the Shroud. The fragment of brown fibril is from a scorch area. (© 1978 by John H. Heller)
Lower right: A red blood shard that has broken off from a blood-caked fibril. Fragments of off-image linen fibrils and debris are in the background. (© 1978 by John H. Heller)

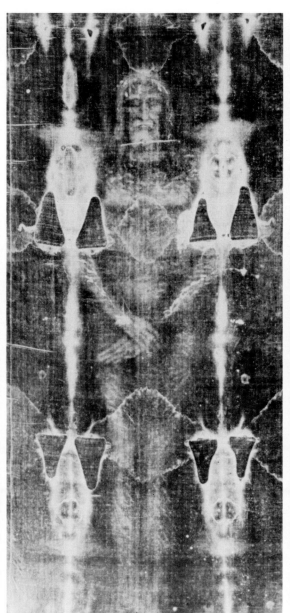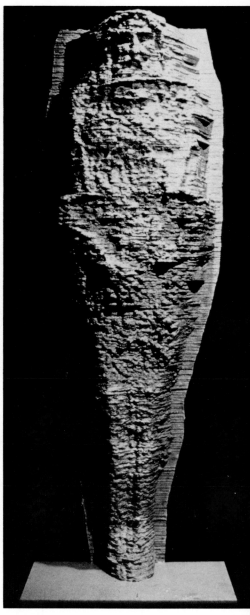

On the left, the frontal image, enhanced photographically, is seen as a positive on this film negative. On the right, a cardboard statue, constructed according to electronic translations of the VP-8 image of the Shroud. Note that owing to the VP-8 all darker features—such as the water stains and blood—appear to be in raised relief. (© 1978 by Vernon D. Miller)

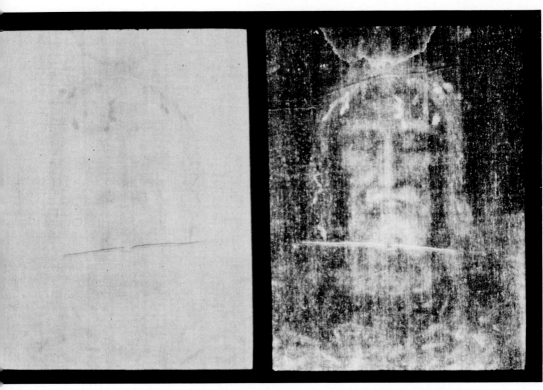

Left: The faint straw-yellow frontal image of the head. It becomes visible only at a distance of 3 to 6 feet, and it fades from visibility at about 30 feet. The horizontal line across the beard is the result of a permanent crease, caused by repeated folding.
Right: On the film negative, the photographically enhanced image of the head is visible as a positive. The white areas on the head are blood flows. Scourge marks can be seen on the upper chest. Above the head is a water stain. (© 1978 by Vernon D. Miller)

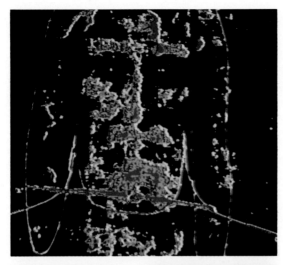

The head of the image as seen in computer pseudo-color, a method used in computer image enhancement to bring out certain features. (© 1978 by Vernon D. Miller)

On the left is an enhanced, full-length photograph showing the negative front and back images. The film negative on the right shows the photographically enhanced images as positives. (© 1978 by Vernon D. Miller)

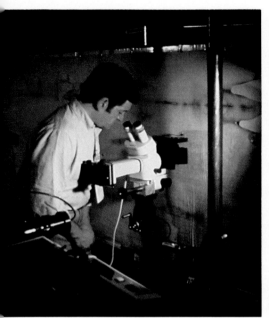

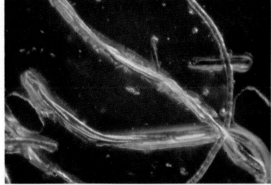

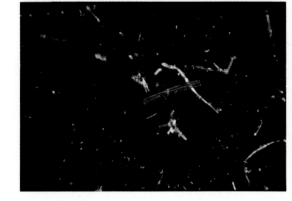

Above: Don Devan examining the Shroud through a macroscope. (© 1978 by Vernon D. Miller)

Top right: Photomacrograph of a bloodstain area of the Shroud. (© 1978 by Mark Evans)
Center right: Background, nonimage linen fibrils from the Shroud. The fragment of brown fibril is from a scorch area. (© 1978 by John H. Heller)
Lower right: A red blood shard that has broken off from a blood-caked fibril. Fragments of off-image linen fibrils and debris are in the background. (© 1978 by John H. Heller)

Microchemistry at Colorado Springs. Jumper on the left, Adler in the center, Sam Pellicori on Adler's left, and Joan Janney facing Adler. (© 1978 by Vernon D. Miller)

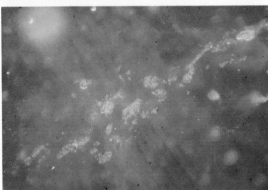

Blood from the lance wound. These globs dissolved in hydrazine give a positive porphyrin fluorescence, positive hemochromagen, positive protein, and positive cyanmethemoglobin reaction. (© 1978 by John H. Heller)

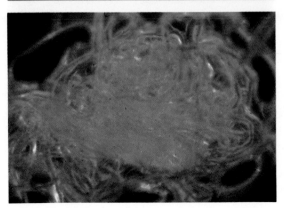

Mass of image fibrils from the back of the man in the Shroud. The colors of the photomicrographs on this and the previous page vary according to the light source used. (© 1978 by John H. Heller. All photomicrographs by William Barrett)

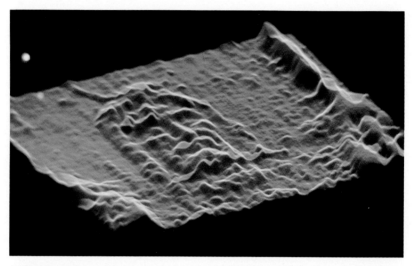

A VP-8 image taken from the instrument's cathode ray tube. The three-dimensional attributes of the VP-8 Shroud images cannot be reproduced by any artistic endeavor. (© 1978 by Vernon D. Miller)

A VP-8 of a photo of William Ercoline. Note the gross distortion of all features and the two-dimensional quality of the VP-8—both characteristic of a VP-8 taken from a 2-D surface. The only exception is the Shroud. (© 1978 by Vernon D. Miller)

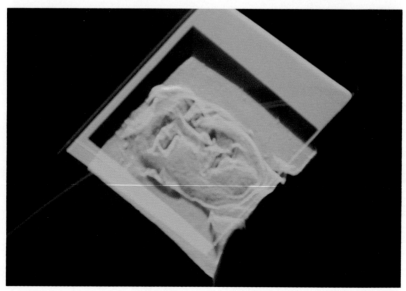

working sense, all attempting to perform dry runs requiring conflicting conditions, in a limited time span, was a recipe for disaster, compounded with catastrophe, submerged in confusion.

In science there are many laws — gravity, speed of light, curved space/time, the uncertainty principle — but all can and may be repealed or modified someday, save one: Murphy's Law. It states that anything which can go wrong will do so. At Amston, Murphy's Law should have risen to the tenth power. It should have been absolute. Everyone knew it. It did not happen. Many wondered about it — if only briefly.

Of course, there were bugs, glitches, and flaws, but new equipment never works properly under any conditions. Instruments have to be calibrated, tuned, and integrated — normally for weeks, often months. Soon, oscilloscopes were flickering, computers were running, X-ray tubes were coming to life, cameras were being loaded, power supplies were humming, optical rigs flared up xenon and mercury arcs. Everyone had immersed himself completely and with the total concentration that such work requires. Jackson and Jumper were fielding scientific questions. D'Muhala, with a clipboard crammed with papers, was arranging travel from all over the nation to New York, and from there to Milan and on to Turin.

I introduced myself to D'Muhala and was told in no uncertain terms that my job — determination of the presence or absence of blood on the samples the team would gather — would begin when specimens came back from Italy. I would not go to Turin, because I would just be excess baggage there. So I passed the time trying to figure out what everyone else was doing.

After about two hours, I began to have a fairly good idea about what everyone was trying to accomplish experimentally. All the investigators were cooperating extraordinarily well. But when I asked questions, I received rather abrupt answers. I was miffed. And I was furious that I was miffed.

I finally wandered into an alcove that contained a bathroom. I looked at myself in the mirror: my brow was furrowed, and the corners of my mouth drooped. I did not like what I saw, and even less how I felt. I took a deep breath and said in the looking glass, "You know, if there's a snowball's chance in hell that this thing isn't a forgery, then you should feel privileged to carry out garbage or do anything else to help. If there ever was a place or time to give your vanity a kick in the backside, it is here and now! Shape up!" I returned to the dry run.

In my peregrinations around the room I encountered Father Rinaldi, and at once felt the immense charm of the man. When Father Rinaldi spoke to anyone, it was as though a 10,000-watt beam of empathy was shining from him. Almost at once, I did not feel alone or out of place.

Then Ray Rogers called me over and said, "John, I'd like to have your opinion on this little write-up I've done. It's what I think the Shroud might be from a chemical viewpoint."

He handed me a three-page, single-spaced, typewritten document. It contained some of the same information that had been in the *Science* article months before. Rogers' review began by stipulating that, for an appropriate scientific study of the Shroud, all possible hypotheses should be stated. Then, after each hypothesis was framed, it must be scientifically tested. The three proposed hypotheses were:

1. The Shroud is a painting.
2. It was produced naturally, by chemicals or volatile products from a body, or fluids produced by a combination of processes involving organic reactions and/or materials.
3. Rapid heating might be the cause of the images.

Those were the three specific possibilities as Rogers saw them. Of course, there was no mention of any miraculous creation or a by-product of Resurrection; that type of thing is totally outside the purview of science. Scientists are in the data business or, as they phrase it, mass, energy, time, and so on. And after all, the Shroud was not a mythic object like the Holy Grail, but an actual linen cloth with images on it. It was made up of atoms and molecules, which science can measure.

Rogers went on to say that if the images were painted (or printed or stained or dyed), they would have been done with colored materials. What colors were available in the fourteenth century, when the Shroud first came to light, or before?

First, they had to be inorganic or organic. These two terms are general convenience categories for chemists. Inorganic materials usually contain a metal salt, like arsenic oxide, zinc sulfide, or sodium chloride. Organic substances contain carbon. These definitions are not absolute, since, for example, a diamond is pure carbon, and most chemists would not call a diamond organic. Organic substances are usually divided into two classes, one, such as protein, starches, and fats, formed by biological processes, the other more usually made by synthesis. However, these definitions are also flexible, and there is a considerable degree of overlap.

Because of the fire that the Shroud had been exposed to, there must have been a temperature gradient, from the hottest portion, where the molten silver burned holes through the folds of fabric, through the area of scorch, to that portion of the linen which was relatively unaffected. The gradient of temperature, Rogers had calculated, went from about 900°C to well below 200°C.

If an inorganic color had been used on the Shroud, it would have had a binder of some type to make the color stick to the fabric. The binders most often used were egg white, gelatin, milk products, and oil. Any of these would have changed color along the line of the heat gradient. But the Shroud showed no color change of this kind, as evidenced by the color photographs that were available. Organic or biological colors could be ruled out by the same reasoning, for anything organic would have changed in hue; it would be darker, lighter, discolored. But there was no evidence of this kind of change, which seemed to rule out the use of any familiar coloring agent.

There was also a serious problem with hypothesis number 2, reactions produced naturally by a body acting on the cellulose of which linen is made. In 1973, when an Italian team examined the Shroud with microscopes, they saw that the color of the images of the man was contained in the crests of the topmost microfibers. Assume that your arm is a single thread of the Shroud. The hairs on top of your arm would be equivalent to the topmost microfibers of the linen. Imagine that the color of the images is confined to the crowns of those arm hairs, with no indication of capillary action nor any evidence of diffusion. That would immediately rule out liquids and vapors. Further, the intensity of color did not seem to vary from one microfiber to the next. The front and back images appeared to have the same intensity of color, even though the body had clearly been lying on its back. Had the images resulted from body chemicals, the back image should have been more intense or saturated than the front one. This also was not the case.

As for hypothesis number 3, that the images were produced by rapid heating, there was no imaginable physical mechanism that could produce a 3-D image by heat.

I read through the three pages, shook my head in disbelief, and started to read through them once more. I decided to walk around the building and see whether that would clear my head. I sat down and read through the pages a third time.

Returning to Rogers, I said, "Ray, this is just impossible!"

Rogers smiled wryly and murmured, "Yes, I know. Now, what I plan to do is to obtain samples for the chemical investigation, including your blood work. The 3-M Corporation has made up some special, clear Mylar tape. One side is a chemically inert adhesive. When we place it on various locations of the Shroud, and apply a known amount of force to the back of the tape . . ."

"How are you going to do that?" I questioned.

"Well, back at Los Alamos they have designed a nifty little gadget that will measure applied pressure." He removed from one of the packing crates a device that could be set to impress the desired number of grams of pressure on the back surface of the tape.

"How do you know how many grams to apply?"

"Ah," said Rogers, "let's do some experiments on the replica Shroud on the table."

We squeezed into a vacant place among the other investigators, and began applying different amounts of force to samples of the tape and peeling it off carefully.

Rogers finally said, "The Shroud, being an old piece of linen, will probably be a lot more fragile than this, so I guess we'd better use one tenth of the pressure we're using here. When I have the tape pulled gently off the relic, I'll mount each piece, numbered and photographed, in this clear plastic box, where nothing can touch the sticky side, so that I can bring it back uncontaminated."

"Who's going to photograph this operation?" I asked. "Brooks or Miller?"

"Neither one. The documentary photography's going to be done by Barrie Schwortz."

I then asked Rogers why carbon 14 dating was not included in the experiments. He told me that as a result of Jackson's visit to Turin, he had received the emphatic instruction from Dr. Baima at the Centro di Sindonologia that any permissible testing must be nondestructive.

Thereupon, Rogers and I began to brainstorm various types of colors that might have defied age and heat and been applied in some strange manner only to the crowns of the microfibers. I reveled in the broad scope and depth of the discussions. We combined our knowledge of ancient techniques for bleaching fabrics, and the use of pigments and stains that had apparently withstood the rigors of history. While Rogers was in Turin, I would remain behind and investigate some of the compounds we had discussed.

Rogers was particularly interested in the possibility of

porphyrins, which I had mentioned to him on the phone when I called him in Los Alamos at Jackson's suggestion. We discussed the matter in more detail, and I told him that a few colleagues of mine at the New England Institute were "porphyrin nuts" and had synthesized and analyzed hundreds of them.

"If it's any of those molecules, we ought to be able to nail it. As a matter of fact, if there's any trace of blood, I can use the specific heme porphyrin in blood to identify it."

I told Rogers that the hemoglobin of blood has as its crucial constituent heme porphyrin, with an iron atom at its center. If we extract the iron, the remaining molecule can be induced to fluoresce a ruby-red by long ultraviolet light. Using this technique, we could readily measure 100 nanograms (a nanogram is a billionth of a gram) of blood.

"If blood is present, we'll find it," I assured him, and added, "I just wish I were going with you."

"You're not coming?"

"Nope. Just one extra body. I guess I'll have to wait till you get back."

"Too bad. It's the chance of a lifetime."

"Yeah, but I guess they also serve who only stand and wait," I found myself saying wistfully.

At this point, D'Muhala decided that it might be useful to know the religious affiliations of the team members. When he took a quiet census, he found that there were six agnostics, two Mormons, three Jews, four Catholics, and all the rest Protestants — Methodists, Lutherans, Congregationalists, Baptists, Presbyterians, Episcopalians, and Dutch Reform. By this time, it was six-thirty in the evening. Scientists at work with their gear in circumstances like these have all the intensity and concentration of a philatelist who thinks he has just found a $100,000 stamp.

According to the schedule, we were supposed to go to supper at a little nondenominational church that D'Muhala had recently joined, after he had decided he would be a theological nonentity no longer.

Jackson and D'Muhala began circulating among the investigators, telling everyone that it was time to go to the bus for dinner.

"Yeah, yeah, in a minute," came the replies from most, and from others, "I'll pass," or "I don't want to eat — I have to get this thing right." For scientists in the mental mode that precedes a major experiment, a minute is tantamount to hours, and it was clear that no one was going to move, come hell or high water. Jackson and D'Muhala stood, perplexed and frustrated.

Suddenly, one of the coincidences that were to follow members of this group, collectively and individually, occurred. There was no storm, no lightning, no reason for it at all, but at that precise moment there was a power failure. All the instruments died, and the lights went out. Obviously, there was no alternative for the team but to grope their way out the door with some flashlights that had been produced. They all boarded the bus, though some members were grumbling about having to go to a church supper instead of a decent restaurant. The idea of any church being involved in a scientific project seemed to be regarded with both overt and covert suspicion.

We had a magnificent dinner and were then asked by our hosts to join them for a service in an upper room that was their sanctuary. There was singing and a brief sermon, in which the minister told us some things that were wondrous strange. As a result of the evening's interlude, a new and unified sense of cohesion was formed in this otherwise disparate group. We returned to the dry run to find the power restored, and we worked well into the morning hours.

· 6 ·

Countdown in Turin

L ESS THAN A WEEK before the team was to leave for Turin,
D'Muhala received a cablegram from the Centro di Sindonologia, asking him to send the twelve-hour protocol.
At the dry run in Amston three weeks before, we had all
recognized that twelve hours would be barely enough time
to do anything except take photographs. D'Muhala immediately called Jumper and asked what to do about the cable.

Eric, who is good at snap decisions, replied, "To hell with
it. Send them our ninety-six hour protocol, and we'll argue
it out when we get there."

The American team had no idea of the political intrigue
behind this cable, or any conception that many at the Centro were virulent anti-Americans. Everyone believed, ever
since Jackson went to Turin in 1977, that the team would be
working under the Centro's auspices. Indeed, at the time
of the dry run, Dr. Baima of the Centro had sent a tape of
welcome, in which he mentioned working with the team.
Two months before the testing, Jackson and Jumper had
sent a letter to the Centro, which said, in part: "It is our
wish that the Church authorities and the Centro, through
the coordinator, Dr. Baima, acquaint themselves with our
program and, likewise, let us know what their directives
will be . . ." Apparently, the Centro's intention was to chop

us off at the ankles, and one of the key architects of this policy was Dr. Baima.

Fortunately for us, the archbishop-cardinal of Turin had enlightened ideas as to how the scientific investigations were to be run, and had thus effectively countered the Centro's bid for control. To begin with, he ruled out any supervisory or regulatory role of the Centro in the experiments. Instead, he appointed two men, a monsignor as the clerical representative and a physicist as science adviser. His choices were superb — and providential from our point of view. The cleric, Monsignor Cottino, was bright, incisive, and tough as nails — all attributes that would turn out to be invaluable. The scientific coordinator was Professor Luigi Gonella, from the Polytecnico, Turin's equivalent of MIT or Cal Tech, and a first-class physicist. Gonella had spent some years in the United States as an exchange professor at the Ames campus of the University of Iowa, spoke English fluently, and was familiar with the American academic scene. The cardinal had full and justified faith in both men and their abilities.

The public exhibition of the Shroud, the three million pilgrims in Turin, the accompanying historical display, and the Shroud Congress that had followed the public viewing, were the high points of the year from the viewpoint of the church authorities. What the scientists would do was almost an afterthought. Prior to our arrival, Gonella had been occupied with his normal academic schedule, and was as unaware as we were of the machinations of Baima and the Centro. Gonella's first inkling of what lay ahead came when he received a curious document from the Centro. It mentioned that Baima and his associates would take samples. Then it went on to incorporate *our* protocol. In our ignorance, thinking that we would be working under the Centro's auspices, we had sent them the entire experimental outline. They had taken the titles of certain experiments, such as X-ray fluorescence, and had grafted onto the names of our teams those of some of their own people. When Gonella

read that, he boggled. He knew these people, and realized they had no idea what X-ray fluorescence was —
or any knowledge about many of the other experiments.
The experiments were in order. The institutions the Americans came from were prestigious. What were these other
names doing on the roster? Something was very wrong.
Then he received further word from the Centro that the
Americans would be limited to twelve hours. Clearly, there
was no way that the experiments could be done in that time.
He decided to wait until the Americans arrived to find out
what they intended. The Centro's plan allotted eight hours
to Baima and his colleagues. The Americans would be limited to twelve. This would leave them time enough to take
some photographs, but the Centro's members would get to
take the samples. Dr. Baima planned to remove threads out
of the Shroud itself. Then, an associate of Baima's from
Switzerland, a "criminologist" named Max Frei, would take
pollen samples. In 1973 Frei had also taken pollen from the
cloth, and had stated that, by using them, he could trace
the Shroud's voyage from Jerusalem, through Turkey to
France, and thence to Italy.

Baima could not fill up his eight hours by taking threads
and samples, so he wrote to an independent researcher,
Professor Giovanni Riggi, asking him to participate and plan
an eight-hour protocol. Riggi is a bright, enthusiastic, meticulous, and innovative investigator. He was delighted, and
on very short notice worked out an eight-hour protocol.
Then Riggi made a key decision. He submitted a copy of
his protocol directly to Gonella, who was impressed and
approved it. This action was to have far-reaching consequences.

Meanwhile, Jumper had a near scrape with disaster. He
was in a large Air Force cargo plane conducting a zero-
gravity experiment at 40,000 feet when a window blew out,
causing explosive decompression. The pilot dived to 10,000
feet, and Eric was smashed against the ceiling, injuring a
cervical disc in his neck. By the time the plane landed, his

right arm was paralyzed. A civilian physician told him he would need immediate surgery. Eric explained that he absolutely had to go to Turin. Wasn't there something that could be done? Reluctantly, the orthopedist said that traction could be tried, but it would not be adequate. Jumper, the engineer, asked for the mechanical details of the traction rig. With them in hand, he reported to the Air Force hospital and requested traction. He was examined and once again told that traction would not work and that if he was not operated on, the paralysis would be irreversible. He begged and pleaded, and was finally allowed to try it for a week. The team would be leaving in ten days. Six days later he walked out of the hospital, fit and well. Jumper the pragmatist has not a metaphysical bone in his body, but he was forced to say "You have to get the feeling that coincidence just will not quit. Phenomenal. Unbelievable."

On the appointed day, team members began to flow from north and south and west to Kennedy Airport in New York. Those farthest away had to rise at 3:00 A.M. to make connections. Many had had to raise money to take the trip, with only the hope of being partially reimbursed later. Many borrowed. Some, by happy coincidence, came into windfalls. One received a large, unexpected, state-tax rebate. Another, looking around for something to sell, found nothing but some stock of a company that had gone bankrupt. A neighbor mentioned that in such cases sometimes, though rarely, a new company is formed and reorganizes the old one. With this slim hope, the team member went to see a broker. And, as it happened, the slim hope blossomed, and the successor company's stock was worth something — though only half of what was needed. That was better than nothing, but he still had to turn in the stock certificates. The press of his affairs prevented him from doing so for a week, during which time the shares had risen nineteen points, and he had enough money — with $4.00 left over.

Another individual who needed money also had a windfall. When he had taken out his car insurance, the agent suggested that he add insurance on his trailer. Since the trailer never left the yard, he was disinclined to do so. However, the agent said that it would cost only $35; he could check it off on the form, and if it was too much money at the time payment was due, he could cancel it. The team member completely forgot about this episode. As he was wondering where in the world he would get the money, a hailstorm hit, with hailstones of extraordinary size. The trailer was flattened. The owner was about to charge it up to bad luck when his wife remembered the arrangement with the insurance company. He checked, found he was insured, and collected $3,200. His trip was paid for.

As plane, car, bus, and train dropped off the fifty-odd scientists, technicians, and support people, the announcement was made that the pope had just died. Would this jeopardize the expedition? No one had a clue. They tried to call Father Rinaldi, the cardinal, and the Centro — unsuccessfully — and decided to carry on and hope for the best.

They boarded the plane, flew to Milan, and, proceeding to Turin, arrived in time to sleep and catch up with their jet lag.

The next morning at 7:00 A.M. they began with an organizational meeting. The plan for the next week was to unpack and set up equipment, do more dry runs, and be ready for the Shroud. There was only one problem — the equipment had not arrived. D'Muhala went into logistical overdrive. He contacted Father Rinaldi, and off they went to Milan — to collide with the Italian bureaucracy. For convenience, the equipment had been consigned to Father Rinaldi. The glitch was that he had not been back in Turin the requisite number of days to qualify again as a Turinese. The bureaucracy was very sorry, but in these circumstances, there would be a sixty-day impoundment before the equipment could be released. Father Rinaldi cajoled, stormed, pleaded, and raged. But there is nothing on earth so obdurate as a bureaucrat who has fine print on his side. D'Muhala and Father Rinaldi returned to Turin with this

bleak report. D'Muhala went to search out every businessman he knew in Italy, and the priest began to pull every
string he had.

It was now that Gonella made contact with Jackson and
Jumper. Cautiously and diplomatically, Gonella asked how
the Italian contingent had been chosen to work on the
STURP experiments. Jackson and Jumper were taken completely aback.

Jackson said, "How's that?"

Jumper asked, "What are you talking about?"

Luigi Gonella said that it must have been his misunder-
standing — but to himself he thought of the Centro volun-
teering personnel — *timeo Romanos et dona ferentes*. Then he
politely inquired how the Americans were going to carry
out all their experiments in twelve hours.

Jumper replied, "We can't, even though we were told that
that's the allotment."

"Well," Gonella replied tactfully, "I'll investigate."

Leaving, he rushed to see Cottino.

"Why," queried the professor of the monsignor, "were
the Americans limited to twelve hours?"

Cottino replied, "Who said they were? How much time
do they need?"

Gonella said that his information came from the Centro.

Cottino said sharply, "This type of decision is mine to
make."

Gonella now knew that he could get approval for the
ninety-six hour protocol, but thought that it might be a bit
tight. He responded, "I believe a hundred and twenty hours
would be satisfactory."

"Fine," said Cottino. "So be it."

Needless to say, when Gonella reported this to the team,
they were jubilant.

However, there was still no sign that the equipment
would be released, although the team members were told
to expect its arrival at any moment. In the meantime, Father
Rinaldi suggested they go to see the area where they would

be working. Adjacent to the cathedral is the royal palace of the House of Savoy. Here Umberto II had reigned until he left the country. The palace is now a national museum, although tourists are allowed access only to part of it.

The surroundings were lush and opulent. The team entered a large courtyard; at one side was a huge portal, flanked by guards with machine guns at the ready. Inside were more armed guards, and the team, surrounded by tourists, was led up great marble staircases with marble balustrades. Statuary and art were everywhere on display. The team members, many of whom had never seen royal splendor before, ascended two flights of stairs that in height were equal to four conventional floors. At the top, the tourists went left, and the team turned to the right, past more guards with more machine guns. While they paused before ten-foot doors, Father Rinaldi announced that this was the princes' suite, the location where the tests would take place.

A more sumptuous laboratory cannot be imagined. The first of seven rooms was a fifty-by-fifty-foot ballroom. The walls were covered by a golden silk damask with a pale green wainscoting with panels outlined in gilt. The ceilings were twenty feet high. Here and there the wall was punctuated with elaborate coats of arms. The windows, ten feet high and eight feet across, were recessed in box frames. There was marble statuary. On the ceiling there were classical frescoes with cherubim and seraphim and biblical scenes.

In the next room, the Shroud would be placed for testing. This room had crimson silk damask walls with wainscoting, and the floors were of magnificent parquet. In each room hung splendid crystal chandeliers. The art had already been removed from the walls and placed on the floor.

In all rooms, in addition to the red damask walls, the ceilings had elaborate Renaissance-style frescoes of biblical scenes, allegorical figures, clouds, sunlight, flying swans, cerulean sky, putti everywhere, and trompe l'oeil in each corner. The furnishings were replete with gilt, silver, and carved woods inlaid with more woods and ivory.

The walls of the last room were covered with tapestries, one of which depicted Don Quixote and Sancho Panza. Team members were divided as to whether it should be regarded as "dreaming the impossible dream" or "tilting at windmills." There is, I think, a distinction.

Finally, there was a lavatory equipped with two toilets and a larger number of sinks. This would be the one and only source of needed water. The team members were caught between dumbstruck admiration of the surroundings and the need to plan experimental layouts, for they finally had a concrete idea of the areas available for allocating apparatus and work space. The Shroud test room was only one-fifth the size they had been told it would be.

It was Rudy Dichtl's job to see that the team had adequate electrical power. Father Rinaldi had submitted a request to the Turinese bureaucracy, whence it may emerge some time after the year 2000. One look at the suite made it clear to Dichtl that the amount of electricity available was totally inadequate. Furthermore, Italian power is 240 volts and 50 cycles. Dichtl and Dee German were ready for this contingency. Dichtl began to backtrack power leads from the princes' suite. He finally wound up going to the bowels of the building and beyond. When he spotted the main Turinese power main, he knew what he had to do. He began walking around Turin to find the type of store he needed. Once he found it, he bought several hundreds of meters of heavy power cable. Returning, he plunged once more into the basement and hooked directly into the main. Then, feeding out the heavy cable, he wended his way back to the building, up the elaborate stairwell, down corridors, through doors. When he finally arrived at the test facility, he was ready to hook up the cable to the necessary converters to give us 120-volt, 60-cycle power — 45,000 watts of it — when and if the equipment arrived.

The space limitations necessitated more meetings and revised procedures. And there was still no progress with the equipment.

Meanwhile, Gonella had received another document from the Centro. They were insisting that each member of STURP sign an agreement stipulating that all scientific results and information be released only through them. Jackson was appalled. He knew that if he showed such a document to the team, with the implicit censorship it contained, the members would pack immediately and leave. He thought fast and dug out of his files the agreement the STURP members had signed in Norwich. Handing it over to Gonella, he explained the situation.

Gonella looked at the two documents, and said slowly, "I see what you mean. I'll get back to you."

Gonella went directly to Monsignor Cottino and related what had just occurred. The monsignor was seriously angry at this further intrusion by the Centro. He told Gonella that the Americans would not be harassed further. Another attempt at sabotage had been narrowly averted.

It was now Wednesday. According to the plan, the team should have been in the third day of rigging gear, calibrating, and checking equipment. The delay was frustrating and infuriating. Father Rinaldi was still waging war with Italian customs. He finally had enough. He called Rome, got through to the minister of commerce, and told him in unequivocal terms that if the equipment was not released at once from customs in Milan, it would precipitate an international scandal. Further, Father Rinaldi would see to it personally that the scandal was known, for he intended to call in the entire press corps and tell them that the minister himself was responsible for preventing the scientific testing of the Shroud of Turin!

That did it — almost. Milan released the gear on Thursday, and it went to Turin, where it wound up in Turinese customs! The crates were to be released as soon as a bond was posted; the sum required was roughly 10 percent of the value of their contents. The team did not have the millions of lire that would cost, nor did they have a clue as to where to get the money. Monsignor Cottino went to the archbishop-cardinal of Turin and explained the problem. His Eminence guaranteed the bond from the clerical account. When I later asked what, exactly, that meant, I was told in simple language that he had hocked the cathedral. And STURP had feared church obstruction!

Friday dawned, and everyone's spirits soared. The vigil began. Then hour after hour went by, and no truck appeared. Frustration coupled with anxiety infected the group. Suddenly, a cry went up: "It's coming!" Sure enough, a large lorry appeared, piled high with crates. There it was — eighty containers, three thousand cubic feet, eight tons' worth of valuable equipment.

Everyone ran down, pushing through the tourists, flagging the truck into the courtyard.

Where, the truckers wanted to know, was the forklift?

"Forklift?" asked D'Muhala. "There is no forklift."

The driver and his assistant explained that so many of the containers were so heavy that they could not be off-loaded without a forklift, and besides, there were no stevedores to carry them from the courtyard up the two huge flights of stairs.

They had not reckoned on the energy of a bunch of fervid, frustrated, frenzied, and frantic researchers. Like locusts, the scientists swarmed over the truck and began unloading. They seized crates and, at a dead run, headed for the palace entrance, roared up the stairs, and into the princes' suite. As soon as one load was deposited, they ran down for more.

The Italians were astonished. Illustrious *professori* sweating like navvys doing menial grunt work, and doing it flat-out — unbelievable! Some of the crates were the size of a sofa and weighed several hundred pounds. Tom Haverty, an infrared man who could have been a linebacker and had no use for tact, seized a huge load and headed toward a group of tourists, shouting, "Get out of the way! Gangway! Get the hell out of there or I'm going to run you over."

He smashed through the crowd while Jumper, who had a hundred-pound load on his shoulder, was laughing so hard, he almost fell over backward.

Neither daunted nor dismayed, the scientists persevered, dripping with perspiration and panting like locomotives. Dr. Joseph Gambescia, the pathologist from Pennsylvania, mused, "It must be some kind of miracle that no one has had a coronary or at least a hernia. This is a virtuoso performance of muscle, speed, and brainlessness."

When the last crate arrived in the ballroom, where they were all piled in the center, an official of the palace museum arrived in a state of extreme agitation. He began expostulating and waving his hands. The team was mystified, and the language barrier prevented communication. The official grabbed a pad and began to sketch. Suddenly, it dawned on the scientists. The supports of the ballroom floor could not carry a dead weight of eight tons in the middle. Horrified, they turned to and, as fast as possible, picked up the crates and distributed them around the floor. The official gave a vast sigh of relief and made a few more drawings. As far as anyone could figure out, it seemed that if that floor had given way, a lot of other rooms would have gone, too. The Americans were so shaken by the possibility of disaster that they decided to bend over backward from then on. This was fortunate, because, as they found out later, museum officials were extremely concerned lest the parquet floors be scored, the wainscoting scratched, the fabric on the walls torn, the art and statuary damaged.

Five days had been chopped out of the schedule by customs, so activity took on a frenzied pace. Hammers and prise bars flew. Everyone knew what to find in which crate, for everything had been logged and catalogued by D'Muhala. The ballroom was set up for repair, maintenance, and logistical control.

Dee German and Rudy Dichtl were now able to hook up

the power. They had gone over the schematics of every device and thought of each component that might fail. They had resistors, capacitors, fuses, spare parts, tools of every type and description. They even had a portable workbench, which they set up. Roger and Marty Gilbert, a husband-and-wife team of optical physicists from Stamford, Connecticut, had brought a large collection of optical replacements. D'Muhala had independently brought even more, including, providentially, two hundred feet of garden hose. These were now rapidly deployed.

The windows were shuttered, blocked, and fitted with thick black plastic. The doors were baffled with black plastic so that no light could leak in. With all these openings sealed off, no fresh air could get in, and for the next five days the carbon dioxide and water vapor rose significantly, making the atmosphere in the room rather ripe. Other rooms were set up as preparation rooms, and they were filled with gear. In these rooms equipment could be adjusted, tested, calibrated, and then brought into the Shroud test room. Ron London, a radiographer who cheerfully clomped his way through the palace in cowboy boots, converted the lavatory into a darkroom so that X rays and some other films could be developed on the spot. One by one the sinks were cannibalized. Tanks were installed; safety lights, water pipes, and electrical connectors were rigged. The X-ray tube had to be water-cooled. When the hoses were rigged, a hundred feet were needed to bring in the water, and another hundred feet to return it. Other hoses and Tygon tubes were fitted, and everything worked out well, save for one return tube to a toilet from one tank. London went looking for D'Muhala. Tom surveyed the situation and saw that about five more feet would be needed — but it was all downhill. He said he would be right back, and then wandered down to the guard room on the first floor. There he saw a stove and had an idea. When the guards were out of the room, he detached five feet of the stovepipe and returned to the lavatory. It worked like a charm. Had the original palace designers seen these transformations, they would have thought the result straight out of Jules Verne. Had any sanitary authorities been privy to the changes, they would have declared the princes' suite a health hazard.

Soon, three dozen electric cables and connections began to snake across the floor in the Shroud test room. Concerned about the parquet floor and worried that the cables might scrape doors, some enterprising soul went out and bought a huge number of disposable diapers. Every metal link and connection was wrapped with black electrical tape and then secured in a diaper. Packing insulation — glass wool — was used to protect doors and walls. Every item that might mar, scratch, or even rub against anything was packaged with the softest and best insulation that could be found. When the museum officials came to express their fear about damage and saw the precautions taken, they positively beamed in appreciation and thanked the team effusively.

As soon as equipment began to be powered up, glitches developed. One of the biggest was in the X-ray fluorescence gear. This is not a single instrument. First there was an electric cable, which came from a power supply to the transformer. From it a 50,000-volt cable went to the tube. Also attached was the amplifier and multichannel analyzer. When the whole apparatus was assembled and the various switches thrown, nothing happened. It was dead: no signal lights, no friendly hum, nothing. All 1028 channels of the analyzer were out. That was the signal for Dee German and Rudy Dichtl to go into their act at full speed. Helping them was Franco Faia, an electrical technician from Turin. The first guess was that the detector might have warmed up above the liquid-nitrogen temperature at which it had to be kept. The truckers, in loading or moving the gear, may have tilted the vacuum flask containing the refrigerant, thus exposing the detector — in which case it was finished. But the men tested every aspect. Dee started with the analyzer. With the circuit diagrams in hand, he passed hour after hour, testing every connection, capacitor, resistor, and component. Finally, he was down to the circuit boards. Either one had been miswired at the factory, or the wrong board altogether had been installed. This never happens — but this time it had.

While the repair crew was working on the components, D'Muhala and others were working at the telephones. They were after replacement parts. They made concentric circles around Turin on the map, moving out to include Switzerland and Belgium, and winding up on the West Coast of the United States. It was night in the New World, but none of the team had any compunction about rousing people out of bed at 3:00 or 4:00 A.M. and pleading for help. The manufacturer, when called, said it had sold similar equipment to the Fiat plant in Milan. Faia got on the phone, dragged an engineer out of a meeting, and asked for help.

Within ninety minutes, the man was at the palace with an analyzer and amplifier in his car trunk. The gear, when carried up, turned out to be similar but not identical. And it ran on 240 volts and 50 cycles. Then Dee, Rudy, and Franco did something I still cannot believe. They hooked up the U.S. analyzer on the 110-volt, 60-cycle line, and the Fiat one on the 240-volt, 50-cycle line. Then they cross-wired the two to by-pass the defective circuit board. And with this haywire rig they were on the air and ready to go — but not for long. In the shuffle, some of the heavy-duty insulating grease had been removed from one of the prongs on the 50,000-volt connector cable. When it was inserted, there was a 50,000-volt short circuit, a crash, and a five-foot flame shooting into the air, leaving the connector so much slag. Unphased, Rudy and Dee cut off one foot of heavy-duty cable and hard-wired the cable into the transformer. While this was proceeding, Faia, draining the oil from the transformer, noticed that one of the electrical windings was burned out. The whole transformer could be rewound — a factory job — or thrown away; there was nothing else to do. Yet in a manner still totally mysterious to all, Faia reestablished electrical continuity and replaced the oil. Then he handed two scientists a fire extinguisher apiece and said,

"Good luck." The switches were flipped on, and this hard-wired, cross-connected, jury-rigged cludge buzzed, burped, crackled — and ran! Faia fainted. All of this madness had taken forty-eight hours straight through to accomplish.

While this breakneck repair job was going on, other problems loomed. Vern Miller had designed a good part of his photography around six dry-cell power packs, which he had shipped independently. They had not arrived. Since this kind had not been manufactured for fifteen years, Vern was sure he could not find replacements in time. Before he could get into a real swivet, he espied a *National Geographic* photographer who was also wedded to this type of power and happened to have a pack, which Miller promptly borrowed until his own arrived, forty-eight hours later.

These narrowly averted catastrophes played hob with Jackson and Jumper's carefully orchestrated schedule. The general test plan for the first forty-eight hours had been as follows:

Hour	Test Group	Number Personnel Required	Time Allocated Hours	Remarks
1				
2				4½ hours
3	Photography	8	6	photomosaic
4	(Block 1)			
5				1½ hours
6				spectral coverage
7	X-Ray Radiography	7	2	Preliminary test
8	(Block 1)			exposures taken
9				
10	X-Ray Fluorescence	6	4	
11	(Block 1)			Foot blood
12				
13	Infrared (Block 1)	6	1	I/R photos test exposure
14	Spectroscopy (Block 1)			Infrared reflectance fol-
15				lows spectroscopy (re-
16	Infrared (Block 2)			flectance and UV fluo-
17		10	7	rescence) location by
18				location
19	Tape (Block 1)			Tape samples collected
20				

Hour	Test Group	Number Personnel Required	Time Allocated Hours	Remarks
21				
22				
23				Complete
24	X-Ray Radiography	7	7	X-ray radiographic
25	(Block 2)			coverage
26				
27				
28				
29				3½ hour close-up
30	Photography	8	6	
31	(Block 2)			2½ hour spectral
32				coverage
33				
34				
35				
36				
37				
38	X-Ray Fluorescence	6	10	Fingers and face
39	(Block 2)			blood
40				
41				
42				
43				
44	Infrared	6	2	Thermographic test
45	(Block 3)			exposures
46	Infrared			
47	(Block 4)	6	3	Infrared photographs
48				

However, Jackson and Jumper had planned for contingencies and could reshuffle people, times, and experiments. There was always a standby team waiting to plug into a time slot if the assigned group wasn't ready, and a backup team to fill in if there was any problem with the standby group.

Jackson and Jumper were to trade twelve-hour watches, with a two-hour overlap to brief one another on the previous shift. German and Dichtl were to do the same. Owing to the delay in receiving the equipment, everyone worked flat-out around the clock to cope with the crescendo of startup, and the plans for dry runs went out the window.

During the previous two days, the conference on the Shroud of Turin had been held, with admission by invitation only. The team could have gone, but everyone was too busy. Dr. Robert Bucklin, however, attended to present a paper on pathology and blood. Baima was to precede him, but for some reason was unready, so Bucklin presented his paper first. Following the applause, Baima arose and angrily stated that Bucklin had said everything he was going to say. There was no point in his giving his presentation. If Baima was hostile to STURP in the first place, this extraordinary episode did nothing to assuage his feelings.

By Sunday night, almost everything was in readiness. The great testing table had been set up. To make sure no microscopic piece of dirt or dust could be transferred from the table to the Shroud, the team covered each panel with the same one-millimeter gold Mylar that had been used on the lunar lander. Along with the STURP scientists, technicians, and logistic supporters, there was Cottino, Gonella, the Italian team — primarily composed of Baima, Max Frei, and Giovanni Riggi, along with their aides — and some Poor Clare nuns. Close to midnight, someone murmured, "Here it comes."

7

The 120-Hour Adrenaline High

DOWN THE LONG CORRIDOR came twelve men — six on a side — supporting at shoulder height a large piece of plywood covered with red silk. Everyone waited with bated breath, wondering how he or she would feel when the silk was pulled back and the Shroud was revealed. It was reverently placed down, and the senior Poor Clare nun pulled back the silk. Not one member of the team felt even a twinge of spiritual awe or emotion.

JACKSON: It looks like a cloth with funny stains on it.

JUMPER: The image is fainter than I thought it would be.

DINEGAR: The blood is a peculiar color.

ROGER GILBERT: It looks the way I thought it would.

And so it went. Then, two thoughts occurred to every STURP member. Each recounts it in almost identical words: "I suddenly realized that this is a historic occasion, and I'm privileged to be here. Obviously, I must do the most meticulous science I'm capable of." Don Lynn thought to himself, "There have even been more Presidents of the United States than our group of scientists. More people have climbed Everest than are here."

At this point, the whole team was riveted by something that they had initially missed. Cottino was busy pulling out old-fashioned, all-metal thumbtacks that fastened the

Shroud to the plywood. After all the dither that everyone had gone through, including using gold Mylar, here were old brass and iron thumbtacks, some of which left stains as they were withdrawn. Robert Dinegar, the physical chemist from Los Alamos, collected the tacks as keepsakes.

Then the Italian contingent went to work. Baima removed whole threads from the image and bloodstained areas, leaving visible marks behind. Jackson winced, for everything we had planned was nondestructive. He thought about one of Baima's trumpeted concerns, that our taking X rays of the cloth would injure it, and shook his head in disbelief.

This was followed by Max Frei's pollen analysis. Frei took out a Scotch tape container like the kind one buys in Woolworth. He had on a pair of cotton gloves that the team had brought. He pulled off a piece of tape with his gloved fingers; the gloves, by the way, had American pollen on them. Without any reference chart, he began putting on pieces of tape and ripping them off.

Barrie Schwortz was recording sound and was taking photographs as fast as he could click the shutter. He recalls, "I didn't believe any of this. Frei turned and asked, 'Is this an arm?' Talk about amateurish!"

At that point, Frei leaned over with his Scotch tape and exclaimed, "Ah, the face!"

John Jackson, usually mild and tremendously tolerant, called, "No!" and turned to Gonella: "I object to this procedure."

Gonella replied, "I can't do anything unless this is an official complaint."

"You have it."

Schwortz has a wonderful photo of Jackson and Frei glaring at one another, with Gonella between them. Gonella listened to the reasons for Jackson's complaint, and agreed with him. Frei stomped out of the room, glowering. The Americans gave a joint sigh of relief.

Then Riggi and his assistants began, and the team cheered

up. Here was a scientist of obvious competence and skill whose technique and quantitation were excellent. His protocols were definitive, precise, and reassuring. He had devised and built, among other things, a microvacuum cleaner, which he used on the surface of the cloth and subsequently on the interior of the silver box in which it was kept. He had a Poor Clare nun cut the stitches that held the Shroud to a linen backing cloth so that he could look and work on the underside. The team urged him to use the fiberoptics they had built for the purpose, which he did. As he finished off the eight hours that had been allocated to Baima's group, the American team swung into action with its carefully orchestrated program.

The activity became much more measured than the set-up procedures, but was still highly intensive. Most of the time, one group was working at each end of the cloth while a third was carrying out a procedure in the middle.

In the background at all times the photographic effort — both scientific and documentary — was being executed. The group coordinator was Don Devan, and the members were Don Lynn, Jean Lorre, Vern Miller, Barrie Schwortz, Ernest Brooks, Mark Evans, and Sam Pellicori. The text of the photographic-test plan began:

Background and Basic Theory:
Three major photographic experiments will be performed:
1. Photomosaic coverage (5.6:1 reduction) will cover the entire Shroud with enough spatial detail to permit computer weave removal and detailed feature analysis. Filtration will be: (a) blue/green/red color separation; (b) UV-reflected for contrast enhancement; (c) UV-transmission over light sources/UV-blocking over lens for UV-fluorescence. Film: Kodak SO-115; camera/lens: Hasselblad/150 mm; lights: Norman 200 strobes (2 units providing cross-field illumination).
2. Photomacro/micrography. Photomacrography will provide approximately 3:1 enlargement of specific areas of interest so that details of fibers can be seen. SO-115 film will permit total enlargements on the order of 100 X. Filtration will be gels (blue

or green) over Sun-Pak strobes to provide contrast enhancement. Camera/lens: Beseler TOPCON/TOPCOR (microscope objective). Micrography will be obtained with Wild microscope with 35-mm camera attachment.

3. Spectrally resolved quad-mosaic photography (22:1 reduction — each image will cover a 4' x 4' region on the Shroud). Filtration will be: (1) B/G/R color separation; (2) narrow band (100 A°) spaced over visible spectrum; (3) unfiltered.

4. Miscellaneous coverages: (a) Portable digital spectrometer readings of features of interest using a circularly variable interference filter spectrometer with a silicon photodiode sensor and digital voltmeter readout. (b) Binocular (opthalmic) microscope (10–100 X) for visual examination. (c) Stereo imaging system for analysis of directional dependence of Shroud coloration. (d) Fiberoptics examination and photography of rear surface of Shroud.

This was followed by six pages of details.

Dee German and Rudy Dichtl were working like Trojans. A radiometer would go; a socket would explode; short circuits would occur. Not all problems were electrical or electronic. Ernie Brooks's tripod jammed. After fooling with it for a while, German found that deep within the tripod support, a plastic collar had broken. With difficulty, he extracted the collar and cemented it together, only to find that the reason it had broken in the first place was that there was no lubrication in the shaft. In spite of the thousands of tools and parts everyone had brought over, no one had thought to bring any oil. After all, you do not have to lubricate electrons. This episode occurred at night, and no stores were open, so he sent over to the hotel for some butter.

"Ernie," he said as he buttered the shaft, "this will stink after a bit, but it'll do the job till we get through."

Vern Miller found that one aluminum rod would not fit into its holder. Dichtl picked up a hammer and began to pound the end down to size.

Vern gasped. "You can't do that; the aluminum will shatter."

"Uh-huh," answered Rudy, and kept on beating until he finished the job.

Those who were off shift stayed to help those who were on. Chemists were helping out physicists, who in turn were aiding photographers. The collaboration was altogether extraordinary.

It was about this time that Riggi decided that he was impressed by the American effort. He asked Gonella if there were any reason why he could not affiliate himself with us. This was the type of science he believed in. Gonella thought about it and told him, "Why not? You submitted your protocol to me as an independent investigator. I approved it. You are therefore not a part of any team and can do what you wish."

The Americans welcomed him with delight.

Whenever exhaustion hit a team member, he or she would try to nap on one of the cots in the brightly lit ballroom. Schwortz could not sleep because he was so entranced by the frescoes overhead. Some would go back to the hotel for a short rest. During the entire five days of the experimentation the average sleep period per person amounted to two or three hours out of every twenty-four. For 120 hours, everyone was on an adrenaline high.

Because of the X-ray developing tanks and pipes, there were no sinks with running water available. Some of the more daring investigators tried to get a drink of water as close as possible to the fresh-water inlet of the X-ray developing wash tanks. Most of the others had to drink the wine provided from time to time by the machine gun–toting guards, and by Gonella from his private stock. Only one toilet in the lavatory was available for the whole gang of men and women, though it was periodically confiscated by Schwortz, who had to set up developing gear to test the quality of his pictures.

Then Roger and Marty Gilbert came on line for a twenty-four hour run with the reflectance spectroscopy. After they had measured the background (the off-image areas), they were to begin at the foot and work up the body to obtain spectra, in the hope of developing some understanding of the nature of the images. Once they obtained the initial series of spectra on the heel, they began slowly to move up the leg. The spectra were totally different. Eric Jumper, who was on at the time, was discouraged. He thought, "If we keep getting different spectra from one part to the next, we will know even less afterward than we do now. How in hell can the same images give different spectra unless they're made of dissimilar materials?" It was a most unsettling thought. By the time the Gilberts had reached one knee, all the spectra were alike, except for the heel.

"What," wondered Eric, "is peculiar about the heel?"

He called in Sam Pellicori, who rigged the macroscope and slid it down the support system until it was right over the heel. He looked at it carefully under full magnification, and after a long examination turned to Eric and said, "It's dirt."

"What?" exploded Eric. "Let me look!"

Deep into and between the threads dirt particles could be seen. Thoughts rocketed through Jumper's mind.

What could be more logical than to find dirt on the foot of a man who has walked without shoes? Obviously, no one was crucified wearing shoes or sandals, so he was barefoot before they nailed him to the cross. There is not enough dirt to be seen visually, so it follows that no forger would have put it there, because artists aren't likely to add things that cannot be seen. It is only because of the anomalous spectra that the team looked at the heel macroscopically. Could it be a genuine grave cloth? What other explanation could there be?

It was a single data point, but Eric and Sam realized it was not a trivial one.

As Pellicori and Evans continued their macroscopic examination, and took photomacrographs of everything with different magnifications, certain salient points became clear.

The body images were straw-yellow, not "sepia," as all the accounts stated. The yellow did not vary significantly in either shade or depth. In short, it was essentially monochrome, with the color only on the crowns of the microfibers of the thread. Where one of these fibrils crossed over another, there was a white spot on the underlying one. Some microfibers looked like yellow and white candy canes, the white area resulting from one thread crossing another and protecting the underlying area from the image-making process. The straw-yellow fibers showed no sign of capillarity — the principle that makes ink spread on blotting paper. If the corner of a blotter is put into an ink drop, fluid is sucked up into it. Liquid goes into polysaccharide fibers (paper, cotton, rayon, and linen) by capillary action. The absence of capillarity is evidence that no fluid was used. By definition, paint has a liquid base. When the base is water, usually a starch or a protein is added as a suspending agent. If, then, paint had been used on the Shroud, the fibers should have adhered to one another and matted together. An oily vehicle would have had the same effect. But neither matting of fibers nor adhesion between them was seen on the Shroud image.

However, wherever there was a bloodstain in the image area, there was matting *and* capillarity, as would have to be the case with actual blood, which is a mixture of water, cells, and blood proteins. Finally, there was no meniscus effect in the images, but, again, there was in the areas where there was blood. A meniscus can be seen in a glass of fluid, such as water. Where the fluid touches the glass, it curves up: this is the meniscus. Lack of it in the images was further evidence that a liquid paint was not used, but its presence in the bloodstained areas posits fluid.

During the entire period of the testing, a representative of the archbishop-cardinal and a faculty member of the University of Turin were always present. Their job was two-fold: to see that no harm came to the Shroud, and to sign the pages of the laboratory notebooks that each investigator kept every day to attest to the findings that were made. After the first two days, these clerical and academic guardians were sufficiently impressed by the team's meticulous care that they were no longer concerned about the Shroud being damaged.

The work did not proceed uneventfully. As D'Muhala said of Tom Haverty, "He's a character. If you're going from here to there, he'll permit one side trip, provided it's not more than two inches — and then he explodes. He goes right out of his skull."

Haverty was having trouble with his infrared film. It was so sensitive to invisible IR radiation that he could find no place dark enough to load it into his camera. One night, with camera and film, he crawled under the Shroud test table in the blacked-out room. When, three rooms away, Miller turned on a light, Haverty screamed, "Aaaaaaargh!" Frustrated, he went into the lavatory-turned-darkroom. For some reason, he stood on top of the open toilet bowl, one foot on each side. Suddenly, he gave a horrendous shriek; he had fallen in. Jumper rolled on the floor.

That evening, a few very tired researchers returned to the hotel, where they sat in the lobby, drinking coffee. A lady approached them diffidently. She was from some English-speaking country, and she asked, "May I talk to you?"

The team had been continuously harassed by reporters of both sexes, and they were gun-shy, but in this case they could recognize the clear agony on the woman's face. She was asked to sit down and was given some coffee — and she began to talk. She had experienced some tragedy in her life and was still in a grief-stricken quandary, the nature of which was never mentioned. Would it be possible, she inquired, for her to send some flowers to the Shroud? It was an unusual request. Admission to the princes' suite was impossible unless one had two badges. One, made by STURP, was color-coded with the photo of the bearer; the other was white, with the signatures of the cardinal and Monsignor Cottino. The guards would pass only those with both badges.

One team member told the woman to bring the flowers to the outside guard and be sure to ask for the STURP man, who would be on duty for the next thirty-six hours. The lady was profoundly grateful. Shortly after, the bouquet arrived, and the roses were duly picked up by the scientist and placed in a beaker of water next to the Shroud. Within a day, the roses began to wilt, and the investigator was about to throw them out when he had a thought. He discarded all but one, which he touched to the cloth and later brought back to the hotel. There he sought out the lady, told her what he had done, and presented her with the rose. She became transformed. Her sorrow-etched face became radiant with joy. Tears filled her eyes, and she could barely stammer her gratitude. No one ever learned the nature of her pain, nor what the resolution was. But that was unimportant. The lady with the rose left Turin with a rejoicing heart, and that was all that mattered.

Not only this woman but all the clerics and Turinese university personnel who came into contact with the Shroud invested with special meaning the act of touching it with some object — with a handkerchief, a card, or some postage stamps. It was as though they felt that something mystical might be transferred from the cloth to the touched object. Or perhaps it was merely a souvenir. I would discover later that this was more the rule than the exception. It was to have considerable significance.

As the work progressed, the recorded results began to pile up. Everything that was done was logged. Some spectra were recorded on magnetic tape; others were plotted out on X-Y recorders; still more were encoded numerically by hand. Everything was photographed. Everybody was photographed. Every action by every person was photo-recorded so that a complete documentary would be available of each individual's action, location of measurement, and instrumentation. A voice recording was made of every event so that there could be no question of what was done when, by whom, and how. There was originally a plan to send some data back by satellite so that it could be mathematized in the home laboratories to determine if more measurements should be made. This, however, did not work out, so everything was stored. Some of the scientists made duplicates of their data to be carried back by two different people in case one set was lost or stolen. The number of data was truly enormous: the X-ray fluorescence research alone produced sixteen thousand data points. Whatever was to be discovered from all this analysis, there would be no lack of specific, reproducible evidence. Regardless of what the data showed, the meticulous nature of the experiments would produce unequivocal data.

So intent was everyone on doing the finest work possible that endless controls, blanks, air samples, and dust samples were run. Everyone knew that this was a once-in-a-generation — perhaps several-generation — opportunity. They knew that people all over the world were interested in what they found, and that any results must be accurate beyond any doubt. In scientific terms, the statistical significance would be huge.

The work progressed until it was time for the $5000-per-roll sticky-tape experiments to begin. There had been considerable discussion as to what kind of adhesive to put on the tape. What was needed was a chemically inert stickum that would not leave a residue on the cloth and yet could pick up samples of anything it touched. After the fire in 1532, the Holland cloth patches were sewn over the burn holes. These relatively modern sections should have been the strongest part of the cloth. However old the rest of it — and the range was from 630 to 2000 years — it should have weakened through the centuries. Linen can survive well in arid areas like the Sahara, but not in the temperate climate of France and northern Italy. Dampness, oxidation, and organisms like bacteria and fungi cause it to decay, become brittle, and break down. The team expected the Shroud to be in a delicate condition. It was not. It was supple, strong, and felt almost like a new, expensive tablecloth. The weave, a relatively tight herringbone twill, had not only right-angle strength, but diagonal strength as well. We were to determine subsequently that, though it was covered with mildew spores, there was no mildew on it. We still have no explanation for this or for its splendid condition.

Robert Dinegar and Ray Rogers, who were going to apply and remove the sticky tape, decided to approach the procedure with extreme caution, in accordance with agreed-on procedure — and in contrast to what Frei had done. If the first take caused even the slightest damage to the cloth, they would immediately abort the experiment. On each selected target spot for tape sampling, a variety of test procedures was done before and after the tape to make sure that no change of any kind occurred in the sampled area. There was no alteration of surface anywhere after the tapes were removed. Samples of every feature were taken. These included the off-image areas, Holland-cloth patches, burn and scorch marks, water-stain margins, inside water stains, image and blood areas, areas at the margins of bloodstains, and scourge marks. Some tapes were taken of intersect areas. For example, some of the water stain intersects nearly every other feature. In short, anything that could be identified was sampled several times from various areas. Wherever a sample was taken, physical measurements were again locked onto the site and recorded on a grid.

Though 120 hours seemed generous at the start, there were suddenly only thirty hours to go, and now, with the time constraint becoming apparent to all, the pace increased. When a problem arose, there would be a hurried conference with Jackson, Jumper, or both. A decision would be reached within a matter of minutes, and the new solution would be acted on. The failure rate of components began to rise, and the replacement parts began to be depleted. Sockets, wires, contacts, resistors, circuits — all began to go.

German and Dichtl's rate of activity rose to a more frenzied level. Franco Faia had to be available around the clock, for he was the only man who knew the location of all the circuit breakers in the palace. Team members had spread out around a two-mile radius to locate any stores, shops, and maintenance facilities where backup components could be obtained.

As the scientists reviewed their evidence, they found segments of data that they wanted to test over. The scientific photographic team, which had been considered most flexible in terms of being moved in and around other experiments, now had to push the throttle to the floor. So did the third block of the X-ray fluorescence. The major part of the thermography had been left for last, since it had the lowest priority. But now Joe Accetta went into overdrive to accomplish it. Everyone wanted to crowd in a few additional measurements to expand the data base a bit. Fatigue and tension lines began to appear in faces.

As the last hours ticked by, Ernie Brooks and Vern Miller began to set up to do very special Polaroids. The film was a brand-new product designed to hold its colors for at least a century. The team had only been given thirty films, each about the size of a chest X-ray. This was the last procedure to be done. Jumper was in a hurry to bring things to a close. He said brusquely, "You have only thirty minutes. Hop to it!"

Ernie Brooks, almost always mild-spoken, retorted, "These Polaroids will be more valuable to your great-grandchildren than you will. Don't be an ass."

When Eric is wrong, he will admit it. So Ernie, Vern Miller, and Barrie Schwortz carried on, and obtained some of the most beautiful, scientifically superb photographs of the lot.

And with that, five frantic days came to an end. There were brief closing ceremonies. A priest said a prayer, bent, and kissed the Shroud. Brooks, a Presbyterian, waited till he was alone with the cloth, and he kissed it too.

Then Cottino, some other clerics, the team, and the guards all assembled, took photographs of one another, and everyone signed one another's photographs. The Poor Clare nuns reappeared, and the Mother Superior, taking a needle and thread, with brisk, efficient motions sewed a new red silk covering cloth to the top of the Shroud. When she finished, she paused a moment and handed the needle as a gift to a very young novice. The girl received the needle, and her astonishment was replaced with a smile as radiant as if she had just been touched by an angel.

The testing was at an end.

8

It's Red but What Is It?
Experiments in
Microspectrophotometry

THE SECRECY surrounding the team in Italy had been so effective that I had heard nothing of its activities. In order to do something to push forward on my end, I asked my wife, Maria, if by any remote chance she happened to have some antique, hand-spun, hand-woven, undyed linen. My wife is a remarkable woman. She has crafted in bronze, copper, stained glass, shells, rattan, and bamboo; has built beds, tables, lamps, and fountains; done masonry, plumbing, lighting, tile laying, not to mention sewing, sculpting, and painting. In her attic she stores an incredible assortment of useless, exotic, impossible-to-find items. Maria went up into the attic and brought down almost a square foot of fabric — antique, hand-spun, hand-woven, and undyed.

"How old is it?" I asked.

"Oh, I'd say about three hundred years."

I just shook my head in wonder. As it turned out, pieces of this fragment of old Spanish linen would be used as control and experimental samples by most members of the team.

I took the cloth to the New England Institute the next day

and had a colleague draw 50 cc of blood from my arm. Letting the blood cells settle out by mild centrifugation, I poured off the plasma and placed drops of blood and plasma on the old linen in different ways. Then I took tape similar to the one being used in Turin and pressed it on both the clean and bloodstained areas of the cloth. I removed the tape samples and, using a variety of microscopic techniques, examined the microfibers that came off in the adhesive. I wanted to familiarize myself with what I might see when I received the Shroud samples. Each day, I spent a few hours looking at this material; in fact, I reached a point where I dreamed about microfibers.

Then it was late November. The team had been back for four weeks, and I still hadn't received word or samples. I called Roger Gilbert. "Hi, Roge. How did it go in Turin? How long did they let you work on it?"

"Great. We had five days and five nights. We were able to complete every experiment, even the lowest-priority ones."

"What did you find?"

"Don't know yet. We're still reducing the data."

"Well, what was your overall impression?"

"As I said, I'm still analyzing the data."

I then called Bill Mottern in Albuquerque. He was equally taciturn and unforthcoming, as was Eric Jumper, whom I tried next.

Then I called Ray Rogers. "Ray, from a chemical viewpoint, what was your impression of the Shroud?"

"Well, it was quite interesting."

Ready to chew battleships and spit nails, I changed the subject. "When," I inquired, "will I get some samples to start testing for blood?"

"Well," said Rogers, "Walter McCrone dropped by shortly after I returned. He asked to borrow the samples, because he said he could identify what the images of the man in the Shroud were made of. So I let him have them."

"All of them?" I asked incredulously.

"Yes," replied Rogers. "He wanted to review them and then determine what made the images."

"You didn't keep any?"

"Only a couple. I told Walter to send you any that might have blood on them."

"Oh," I muttered, nonplussed.

"Walter's a good man. I've known him for about thirty years."

"Yeah. I know of his work, too. He's the one who debunked the Yale Vinland map."

"He should be sending you some slides fairly soon."

I could not believe it. No researcher *ever* gives out *all* his material. I had written emphatically to Rogers on the subject before the team left for Turin. One of the earliest lessons I had learned in my research career was to guard samples with a passion identical with that of an art collector who has acquired a heretofore unknown Rembrandt. I was deeply disturbed.

Walter McCrone, no matter what his reputation, could be struck by lightning or be involved in an automobile crash. There were any number of bleak scenarios.

In forensic cases, whenever there is a sample to be used in evidence at a trial, the material must be in the possession of a responsible agent. If it has to go to a laboratory, the FBI agents, the police, or somebody reliable will hand-carry it to the laboratory director. If the evidence is out of the possession of a responsible agent, even for five minutes, the attorneys for the other side can claim that the chain of evidence has been broken, and demand that it be excluded from the trial. I had received material hand-carried by detectives from a thousand miles away. Shroud material was a lot more precious, for there would probably never be another opportunity to obtain more samples. Rogers should have cut each tape sample in half, and let McCrone have some half-samples. However, since there was nothing to be done, I forced myself to put the matter by.

After the start of the new year, I called Rogers again to

say that I still had not received anything from Walter McCrone. He told me to call McCrone directly, which I did several times. He was never available.

While waiting, I turned to another aspect of the Shroud chemistry. Could the "blood" be an unusually long-lasting heat-resistant colorant? In antiquity, a rather remarkable dye was made from certain seashells of the *Murex* family. Found in greatest concentration around the ancient Phoenician city of Tyre, it was called Tyrian purple, and reputedly lasted for centuries. When Alexander the Great conquered Persia, and captured the Persians' treasury, he was much taken by the robes dyed with the Murex stain. The conqueror had been told that the robes were two hundred years old. Impressed, he decreed that from then on, this would be the royal color — or so the story goes.

Pliny had described Tyrian purple as ranging in color from a deep purple through amethyst to the color of shed blood. The bloodstains on the Shroud might turn out to be the red variant of the Tyrian purple. I checked ancient references, spoke to authorities on conchology (the study of shells) and malacology (the study of mollusks). After speaking with seven of them, I garnered a lot of information — but nothing on Tyrian red. I tried invertebrate biochemists, with no better luck. Mulling over my lack of progress, I contacted curators of ancient textiles at several major museums. They knew of a light pink from marine sources, but nothing red. Finally, I consulted Professor Max Saltzman of UCLA. He was the ultimate authority on ancient fabric colors.

"There are," he said unhesitatingly, "no deep red, blood-red, or any similar red dyes from marine sources."

When Max Saltzman makes a statement like that — believe it!

That left me with Pliny. I thought a while and finally called Dr. George Ruggieri, director of the New York Aquarium, a marine biologist, naturalist, and classics scholar. When the whole lugubrious story was explained to him, he laughed and said, "John, don't worry about Pliny;

he lied a good deal. There's no Tyrian red and never has been."

"You're kidding!"

"Nope. What he didn't know, he made up."

That was the end of that. Another exercise in futility. Scientific research is filled with such dead ends, and it is in this way that the scientific enterprise proceeds. We investigate possibilities and rule them in or out. At the end, what is left is probably the truth.

I turned to a request from Rogers. One was for the leaf, stem, and root of *Saponaria officianalis,* or common soapwort. Two thousand years ago, it reputedly had been used, together with ashes, to bleach linen. Around A.D. 600 the method of bleaching was changed. Soapwort, then, might provide a crude method of dating the linen. Since it was winter, I called the arboretum of the Smithsonian, and obtained samples. Next, Rogers wondered whether I knew a source of pollen samples of flowers that grew in the Holy Land. If he had such pollens, he said, he might be able to make a correlation with pollens found on the Shroud. Other than writing to some pollen expert at a university in Israel, I couldn't think of a way to reach a readily available source, and mentioned the problem to Maria.

She disappeared into the attic again and reappeared with a small 1925 volume containing pressed flowers from the Holy Land. I shook my head in wonder.

"One of these days, I'm going to ask you for a box of quarks and a test tube full of tachyons, and you'll win the Nobel Prize."

She smiled.

One day, McCrone called and said, "I'll send you a slide that's supposed to have some blood on it, but it's so small, I don't think you'll be able to do anything with it."

I asked incredulously, "Is that all you're sending?"

"What more do you need?"

"I should have at least a couple of other slides to orient

me. At this point, I don't have a clue to what anything looks like."

"All right, I'll see what I can do."

Two weeks later, a small package arrived from Chicago. Excited, I opened it and found a slide container with four microscope slides in it. On each slide the Mylar had been placed sticky surface down and covered by a glass cover slip.

One was labeled "Blank" and was merely an empty piece of Mylar tape, stuck onto the glass. The second was "Scorch." The third was labeled "Nonimage," meaning part of the Shroud that had nothing on it, and the final one was "Blood." On this slide, McCrone had made a circle around a part of the cover slip and had written "Good Luck" on it.

I looked at the "Blood" slide first. I could not believe what I saw or, more precisely, what I did not see. At 1000 X magnification, the piece of "blood" was still a speck. Even under the greater magnification of oil immersion, it was impossible to tell what I was looking at. It could have been blood, dirt, a fragment of a linen fiber — anything. It was far too minute for me to try a blood test, and could not have weighed more than a few picograms (a picogram is a thousandth of a billionth of a gram).

I began to dictate observations, just as though this were a forensic case and I was marking and describing evidence. I described the microscope-slide container, each slide, its condition, how it had been put together, and so on. I noted that when Rogers had brought back the Mylar tape samples, they were in a container built so that each stood vertically, with nothing touching the sticky surface, so as to prevent contamination. All had been hermetically sealed in a clear plastic box to preserve their surfaces from any adventitious material. McCrone had put them sticky side down on microscope slides and covered them with thin glasses. As each slide was placed under the microscope, first at 30 X, then progressively at 100, 250, and 500 X magnification,

I dictated what I saw in each field. Then I looked at the "Blank" slide, which should have given a good indication of whether any recent contamination had touched the sticky surface. I expected to find it relatively clean. It was not. There was a variety of particles of different shapes, sizes, and colors. There were also a few fibers. This was disturbing.

Next to be examined was "Scorch."

"Well," I thought, "this is what I've been waiting for. Actual microfibers from the Shroud of Turin."

What I saw there was disappointing. There were old linen fibers that had indeed been charred. The degree of heat was obvious. Some fibers were charcoal-black, others were brown, and still others were lighter, but all clearly had been subjected to heat. Also obvious was evidence of the debris of ages. This was logical. Old prints had shown literally hundreds of clergy and other officials, each holding the Shroud; it had been handled, kissed, hung, suspended vertically, laid out flat, and so on. There were animal hairs, wool, silk, and cotton fibers, insect parts, wax splatters, pollen spores — the list was long. If the Shroud was older than 630 years, possibly up to 2000 years, there would be no way to tell what debris belonged to what age, with a few notable exceptions. For example, green polyester was obviously modern, and so were other synthetic fibers. Fly ash is also relatively modern.

I turned to the last slide, labeled "Nonimage." There I found very old linen fibers that were uncharred. They had the same debris as the previous slide, but appeared to show nothing else. As I swept the field from side to side, I suddenly stopped. There, beneath the objective of the microscope, was a single microfiber with a coating on it. It was garnet-red.

"That," I said to myself, "sure looks as though it *might* be blood."

It was nearly the end of the day. I placed the slides back in the slide box and locked it away in a safe to which only

I had access. I went to the blackboard in my office. If what I had seen on the last slide was blood, and it had coated only the outside of the microfiber, just how much would it weigh? This was a crucial calculation. I knew I could measure 100 nanograms of hemoglobin with relative ease. If I pushed technology to the limit, I might be able to go down by a factor of ten. If I worked at it, I might possibly get as far as one nanogram.

I made approximate calculations of the density of old, dried blood, the circumference of the microfiber, and the length of the fiber. The results were discouraging. My most optimistic estimation came to a weight of 100 picograms. If what I had seen was, in fact, blood, would it not be the pinnacle of frustration not to be able to measure it?

"Damn, damn, and triple damn!" I thought on the way home. "If you can see it under the microscope, there has to be a way to measure it. I hope."

I remembered talking to Rogers at Amston. What was it I had said?

"If it's any of those molecules [heme porphyrins], we ought to be able to nail it."

I had put my foot in my mouth, and it looked as though I might choke on it.

The next day was Saturday. Like those associated with any research institution, my colleagues and I worked a five-day week, but experiments follow a timetable of their own. Animals must be cared for; some instruments have to be nurtured on liquid nitrogen; marine biological cultures must be monitored and measured. Weekends, nights, holidays — the scientific enterprise never stops. Today there were more cars in the upper parking lot than usual on a weekend. I went into my office, put on my lab coat, opened the safe where I had put the Shroud specimens, and removed the slide on which I had seen the red coating. I clumped down the corridor to the microscope laboratory, removed the dust cover from my favorite Leitz scope, turned on the tungsten light, and fired up the xenon arc — two different forms of transmitted light used in microscope work. Then I inserted appropriate optical attachments for reflected light use as well. Now I had four modes of illumination at my disposal.

At once, I located the fiber I had seen the day before. It did indeed look like blood — very old, but blood.

I decided to see if there were any biologists or medics around, but there weren't. Left to my own resources, I resolved to scrutinize every square micron of the surface of that slide which was supposed to have nothing on it.

Fifteen minutes later, I found another garnet-red fiber.

"Yah-hoo!" I yelped.

A technician working at another bench was so startled that she dropped and broke a Petri dish full of liquid on the floor. I was definitely not a "yah-hoo" type, and she must have wondered what had triggered the outburst. The search continued. In another two hours I had found five more red fibrils. There were now seven microfibers with red stains on part of their length. In addition, I had found one glob not associated with any fiber. It looked to me like biltong — the sun-dried meat prepared by some African tribes I had once stayed with. Though I was sure I had not missed anything, I restudied the entire slide once again. No, there was nothing else. Placing the slide back in the safe, I went to the blackboard in my office to perform some more calculations. I knew the diameter of the linen fibers, as well as the length of those that had the red color on the surface. Though I did not know the thickness of the red coating, I made some reasonable approximations.

While most people seem to believe that scientists calculate down to the accuracy of a dandruff particle on a gnat's eyelash, this is seldom done. Most investigators are quite content to work within "an order of magnitude," which means a factor of ten. For most purposes this is perfectly adequate.

My purpose now was to estimate the total amount of hemoglobin represented by those seven partly coated microfibrils. An order of magnitude would be good enough for the first go-around.

As the math progressed, I became more and more dour. The figure I came up with was approximately 700 picograms of hemoglobin. I knew I could measure 100 nanograms, and possibly even 10, but a picogram is one thousandth of one nanogram. This was going to be one unadulterated stinker of a problem. Sitting at the desk, I looked at the blackboard and brooded. Maybe the math was off. Recheck it. The numbers still came out 700 picograms, excluding "biltong," which I was not sure about.

I decided to go home and forget about it, hoping that somewhere back in my brain the stewing subconscious would give me some new, brilliant insight.

Trying to measure 700 picograms of blood was ridiculous. I am reasonably sure that no one in the history of science ever tried or even fantasized about it. Forensic scientists normally do not even consider anything below micrograms — and they are the only folk who do worry about small samples. Usually, if there is *any* blood, there is plenty of it.

There are many porphyrins in nature, and all do specific jobs for the plant or animal in which they reside. Chlorophyll, for example, contains a porphyrin without which photosynthesis cannot occur. The key chemical structure that I had to measure was heme porphyrin. Heme porphyrin is what enables hemoglobin in red blood cells to pick up oxygen in the lungs and transport it throughout the body. It is also responsible for the transport of carbon dioxide from body tissues and the carrying of this gas to the lungs, from where it is exhaled.

A group at the New England Institute had been interested in natural porphyrins and had successfully synthesized several hundred new ones. Although a porphyrin is an organic chemical structure, the single metal atom in its center makes it a metallo-organic. In blood the atom is iron. If someone's diet is deficient in iron, his body cannot synthesize enough heme porphyrin. This condition is called anemia.

In order to measure blood porphyrin, I would have to use chemical methods that tease the iron atom out of its porphyrin ring. Once that was accomplished, I could use a method from physics that would enable me to (a) identify the porphyrin as being derived from hemoglobin, and (b) measure how much was present. To do this, I would have to irradiate the molecules with long-wavelength ultraviolet light, which would create a red fluorescence. Less than 100 nanograms of testable material would produce too little fluorescence to be picked up by even the most sensitive instrument available in 1979.

There is one instrument, however, that is a lot more sensitive than anything physicists have dreamed up, and that is the retina of the human eye. Years before, I had worked with a group of physicists at Yale to find out how much green light the eye could see. Green is the wavelength (540 nanometers) to which the retina is most sensitive. When we sat in the dark for about thirty minutes to adapt our retinas to the dark, we were able to measure that the best eyes could pick up about 5 to 50 photons of green light. A photon is a single quantum of light. Heme porphyrin without its iron atom is located at the red end of the spectrum. I now estimated the lowest number of red photons that the human eye could discern.

I began to experiment on the old Spanish linen with blood on it. I took some Mylar sticky tape, pressed it on the cloth, pulled it off. Then I treated the surface of the tape with the necessary chemicals — hydrazine and then formic acid — to get rid of the iron in the heme porphyrin. When that was done, I entered the photographic darkroom and sat there for thirty minutes. I switched on the long ultraviolet and peered at the sticky surface of the tape. I swore for thirty seconds without repeating myself. The adhesive used on the Mylar was supposed to be inert. I growled, "Inert adhesive, my foot. It is damn well ert!" It fluoresced blue-white. I knew I would never be able to see red dots against that bright background.

Research is fun when you get an idea and when you finally prove it. In between it is dog work, tedium, frustration, repetition, calibration, measurements, fixing instruments, eliminating glitches, developing computer software, boredom, irritation, bafflement, disillusionment, setbacks, and always, but always, Murphy's Law. To get the fun, you have to put up with the "in between." It seems that it is a law of nature.

I began again. This time I placed a Spanish linen thread covered with blood under a low-power microscope. With a microtweezer, I pulled out microfibers. They were covered with red. Carefully, I placed five of these in a spot well — the technical name for a round dimple in an enamel plate. I added a drop of hydrazine and another of formic acid. I took the plate into the darkroom, waited a half-hour, and turned on the ultraviolet. Nothing! I sighed and returned to the lab.

I repeated the previous experiment, but took out a hundred microfibers with blood on them, and then added the reagents. This time I could barely perceive the faintest possible pink glow from the liquid chemicals.

Relieved that at least *something* was visible, I realized that the red fluorescence had been diluted by the volume of the two drops of added reagents.

How could I add liquid reagents without liquid? Perhaps I could add the hydrazine and the formic acid in their gaseous forms. That might solve a lot of problems: the porphyrin would stick to the fibrils where it was most concentrated, and the reaction might take place on the surface of the fibrils.

I prepared ten groups of bloodstained microfibers. Each one contained fifteen fibrils. In the physical chemistry lab, I had prepared two small chambers in which the spot well could be placed. The first chamber was saturated with hydrazine vapor, and the microfibers remained there for three hours. After that, they were placed in the formic acid–saturated chamber for another three hours. At the end of that period, I took the spot well into the darkroom once more, waited, and flipped on the UV. At first I saw nothing. After about five minutes I perceived three tiny needle-points of red. "Why not ten?" I asked myself. "Probably because there was more hemoglobin on the fibers in three of the piles of fifteen each." I kept staring, but no more red dots appeared on the Spanish linen fibers.

I was looking easily at *fifteen times* as much heme porphyrin as I had available to me on the Shroud fibers — about 10 nanograms. That was about one order of magnitude better than I thought I could do when I started. But it was still an order of magnitude poorer than I needed. Could I develop some technique to improve detection by another factor of ten?

I called Ray Rogers to discuss what I had been doing. "Ray, if this stuff that I'm looking at is blood, and it's on a nonimage area, there must be some more of it around on some slides."

"John, I marked the slide on which I believed there would be blood, and Walter McCrone has it."

"He sent me one slide on which there was a piece of something barely a micron in diameter. He labeled the slide 'Blood' and 'Good luck,' and that's all I have of a so-called blood slide. The seven fibrils are on a nonimage slide."

Rogers answered, "Well, McCrone has the whole lot. If he says that only one slide has blood, and only one micron's worth, maybe that is all we've got."

I called McCrone and left a message, requesting any other slides that had or might have blood on them.

Twenty-four hours later I called McCrone's laboratory again. The woman on the phone said the answer to Dr. Heller's question was no.

Then a colleague, Professor Alan Adler, popped into my mind. I had worked with Dr. Adler on various projects over the years. He would admit to being a physical chemist, thermodynamicist, and a porphyrin nut. He is a Renaissance man, with an encyclopedic knowledge of the physical and biological sciences, military history, ecology, and many other fields. I wondered whether he would be interested, and I decided to approach him sideways.

"Al," I said enthusiastically, "how would you like to get involved in a real fun project? It even involves porphyrins."

"Oh yeah? Did you say fun project?"

"Yup. It might turn out to be the most fun you've ever had on a problem."

"Sounds interesting. Are you guaranteeing it will be fun?"

"Definitely."

We made a date and subsequently rendezvoused in my office.

"All right," said Adler, "enough of this mystery. What's this all about?"

"Have you heard about the Shroud of Turin?"

"The what of where?"

I recounted in detail the nature of the project and all the information I had thus far obtained.

"Do you mean to tell me you have some of those microfibers right here, and you think there's blood on them?"

"Yup. But I can't figure out how to measure it yet."

"Let me see," said Adler, a predatory light gleaming in his eye.

We went into the microscope lab. I put the slides on the microscope and demonstrated the blank tape, the one-micron-of-nothing slide, the scorch, and finally the off-image tape at the coordinates of a microfibril with the garnet-red color.

"John, that's blood!"

"I think so too. But what I haven't figured out is how to prove it."

I showed Adler the other six fibrils and the biltong. I showed him the Spanish linen and the slides made from it. By this time Adler was hooked. We began to repeat all the experiments I had done before, and then to break new ground. We refined the techniques, optimized conditions, tried variations and modifications, and still could not increase the sensitivity or come up with a method for quantification. Adler cleverly devised a way to concentrate the heme porphyrin from the Spanish linen microfibrils into a capillary tube filled with silica gel. But no matter what we tried, the attempt to measure the 700 picograms of heme porphyrin on the Shroud fibers appeared hopeless.

At this point our investigation had to be suspended. It was time for the first post-Turin meeting of the STURP team. Aside from the fact that I had found seven microfibers with garnet-red color on them and a piece of biltong, I had nothing to present. I arranged to have microphotographs made of my slides, both the Spanish linen and the Shroud samples, and with that I packed up and left.

9

Santa Barbara:
The Iron Oxide Controversy Begins

THE BROOKS INSTITUTE OF PHOTOGRAPHY invited the Shroud group to hold its first post-Turin meeting in its facilities at Santa Barbara.

Since the Shroud research was a spare-time activity, done on weekends, nights, and vacations, the meeting was called for a weekend. Everybody — even those from clear across the country — had to be at work the following Monday morning. This gathering, like others held subsequently, was characterized by an intense interchange of scientific information. No one was the least bit preoccupied with what the Shroud was or might be. Data were at issue here; conclusions might come later.

The first presentation was on X-ray fluorescence. I felt like a bird dog at the point, waiting with barely restrained impatience. If paint had been used on the Shroud, the likelihood was overwhelming that the pigments were inorganic, and X-ray fluorescence would tell the tale. X-ray fluorescence could identify any of the dozens of inorganic pigments made up of such elements as arsenic, cobalt, and mercury, available in the Middle Ages.

Roger Morris, a physicist from Los Alamos, presented the paper. He began by describing his experimental equipment and the procedures he used. One of his coauthors was Larry Schwalbe, who had done postdoctoral work at Heidelberg, and would turn out to be a key man on the X-ray fluorescence team. Often described as a "wild hare," Larry is a painstaking, rigorous investigator. His extremely critical demands on himself and other members of the team would occasionally cause gritting of teeth and bouts of profanity, but no one bore him the least ill will. There can be no argument with demands for precision and excellence.

Finally the results were presented. There was calcium on the Shroud — lots of it. It was evenly distributed over the entire length and width. I wondered where in the world it could have come from. It was not concentrated in the image areas, so it couldn't have anything to do with paint, dye, or stain.

Next, they found strontium — also evenly spread all over the linen, but in lesser amounts than the calcium.

I thought this was peculiar. There is not a great deal of strontium in the environment, but it is so similar in its chemical properties to calcium that it is often found wherever calcium is — in milk, for example. If strontium was also distributed throughout, it couldn't have anything to do with the images, either.

Finally, they found iron. Iron was spread uniformly over the whole Shroud *except* in the bloodstained areas, where there was a significantly higher incidence of iron than elsewhere.

"Well, well," I thought. "That's presumptive evidence that the 'blood' may be real blood. The iron atoms in heme porphyrins would account for the extra iron in those areas. I *have* to figure out a way to test the garnet-red spots."

No other elements measurable by X-ray fluorescence had been found. I did not know whether to feel disappointed or delighted. Intellectually, I was betting the Shroud was a forgery. But with no measurable amount of inorganic material in the Shroud image — and with Ray Rogers' insightful thermal analysis, which seemed to preclude organic and biological substances — what were we left with?

"Zilch!" I thought, "a big, round, fat zero!"

At a later meeting, when Jumper was reviewing the X-ray work and Rogers' conclusion, he said to the team, "I've got it."

"You have?" asked Don Lynn.

"Yes. Absolutely. We have just proved that the Shroud doesn't exist!"

Shouts of laughter from all. But in terms of the physical data available, it almost made sense.

Next to present data was Don Lynn, from the Viking team of the Jet Propulsion Laboratory. Don, with his white, New England–fisherman beard, went into a detailed image analysis. He reiterated that the images were directionless and therefore could not have been painted by human hand. He showed slides wherein the computer dropped out the weave of the cloth, leaving the images minus the texture of the linen. He had had a limited time to work on the problem, considering the demands of the space program. He and Jean Lorre had done microdensitometer readings on many of the photographs, four million points for each one. The digital data were processed through an analog device and displayed on a television screen (cathode ray tube, or CRT). It turned out that, though the photographs were visually superb, the computer was picking up the spot where the photographic strobe flash, reflected from the surface, had created a hot spot. To overcome this Lynn and Lorre "stacked up" a large number of images in the IBM 371/58 computer and found that the strobe had moved around as the photographers changed their vantage points. They instructed the computer to subtract the hot spots, creases, and the like, which it obligingly did. When they examined the resultant picture, they were able to determine that the supposed pigtail on the back image and the reported chin bandage on the front were artifacts. They could demonstrate that an occasional new thread of a different diameter, used when the linen was woven, caused these apparent shade differences in the cloth. Because the threads were hand-spun, this was not surprising. The computer also showed what appeared to be an elliptical lesion at the top of the flank blood flow area, which was not visually apparent on the photographs. However, this narrow ellipse is completely consistent with the post-mortem appearance of a wound in the flank made by a thin blade. Finally, in the eye sockets, where the VP-8 had shown something, they found an increased image density.

John Jackson rose and discussed the VP-8 image. He presented mathematical models which demonstrated that there was a single global-mapping function involved. This means that the Shroud-body distance, the drape of the cloth, and the frontal image could be explained only by a single mathematical statement, which stipulated that the Shroud had overlain a body. The back image indicated that a body had rested on that portion of the cloth. Along with the nondirectional quality of the images, the results of the X-ray fluorescence, and Rogers' evaluation, this significantly reduced the possibility that the Shroud was a painting.

At this point there was a break for coffee. The buzz of conversation rose to the level of a hive of bees on a bright summer's day.

When everyone reconvened, Roger Gilbert presented his data. He had designed an ingenious piece of gear to do reflectance measurements. It had both a xenon- and a mercury-lamp source, and produced wavelengths of light ranging from ultraviolet to infrared. These different bands of the spectrum were used successively by increments, and whatever was reflected back was then measured. Reflectance measurements are seldom the methods of choice, because of scatter and anomalous dispersion, but when one does not have any other means, due to the nature of the object and the need for nondestructive testing, it's the best available option. We were shown dozens of slides of reflectance-versus-wavelength curves. There was far too much information for us to digest at one sitting, but one fact did become clear: the color of the lightest scorch area was similar to the color of the images of the man. What this meant, I had no idea.

I couldn't make sense of the measurements done in the blood areas, since I had never seen blood data graphically presented in this manner. I was very familiar with what absorption curves looked like, but had never worked with reflectance curves before.

It was now my turn. I rose and, by waving my hands a lot, managed to use up ten whole minutes. I had seen seven microfibers with something on them that looked like blood, and one piece of biltong. I showed two slides, one of a garnet-red nonimage microfiber, and one of Spanish linen with my own blood. The five-minute question period was consumed by requests from various team members for pieces of Maria's Spanish linen, with and without blood, to use in their control studies.

Following my presentation, McCrone came to the lectern. Everyone was eager to hear what he had to say. He began. He had examined some of the Shroud fibers and stated that the body images had been made by red iron-oxide earth pigments.

Iron oxide is familiar to everyone as rust. It occurs in the ground in a variety of geological deposits, and has been used for millennia as a paint. African tribes like the Masai still use it to daub their bodies and their hair. The painter's pigment known as Venetian red is made of it.

McCrone is a particle expert who has written a five-volume atlas that is the definitive work in this field. Nevertheless, Sam Pellicori, who came to the STURP project via astronomy and physical optics, was at that moment thinking, "I don't believe this. I've measured the spectrum of iron oxide dozens of times. The color's totally wrong for what he's claiming. Based on spectrophotometry and the X-ray fluorescence findings, there's no way that the Shroud images are composed of iron oxide. I may be young and naive, and McCrone may be the master, but he's wrong."

Jackson was thinking that McCrone's analysis contradicted the Gilberts' reflectance curves.

McCrone stated that, in his opinion, the iron oxide had been applied by a finger, and the pictures were therefore finger paintings. He referred to what he had seen as "snow fencing," indicating that the iron oxide had piled up on the lee side of the fibers. He concluded by saying that the blood was also made up of an iron-oxide paint.

Slide after slide was projected on the screen, with McCrone pointing out red dots on the fibers, and stating that they were typical red iron earth pigments.

I was bewildered. Here was a particle expert claiming that (a) the images were the result of iron-oxide red paint and that (b) the "blood" was iron oxide, too. This was completely at odds with the data presented by the X-ray fluorescence team, who saw no increase of iron signal between image and nonimage areas, but only where there was blood. It was at variance with what Lynn and Lorre had found in their image analysis, as well as the Gilberts' analysis that the images had a spectrum similar to the light scorch areas. It also left the 3-D aspect of the images unaccounted for. My seven microfibrils may not have held blood, but they surely were not coated with iron oxide. Most confusing.

McCrone finished up by stating that he was 90 percent sure that the Shroud was a painting — or perhaps there may have been a very faint pre-existing image that was later touched up by an artist using red iron-oxide earth pigments.

I had a flock of questions to ask. However, before I had a chance to ask any, other team members stepped in.

"Dr. McCrone, how do you know those red dots are iron oxide?"

"Experience."

"Did you test them chemically?"

"I don't have to. Experience. Besides, it's birefringent."

"How do you explain the X-ray fluorescence studies and the Gilberts' curves?"

"They must be wrong."

"How does your iron-oxide paint jibe with the negative image and the 3-D information?"

"Oh, any competent artist could have done that."

"Do you mean that you just looked through your microscope and, without doing specific tests for iron oxide, can proclaim it a painting?"

"Yes."

And with that, he left the meeting, and I did not see him again.

McCrone had said that the red dots showed birefringence — a property of certain materials, such as topaz or calcite, where transmitted light is "split" in two directions. This would turn out to be a pivotal point.

I was a new member of the team, and felt I should probably keep my mouth shut, but I thought that McCrone, in spite of his reputation, had stuck his neck way, way out.

What would the public think? They would have no way to judge a dispute among scientists. *That* would be a terrible devil's brew. The whole episode had so perturbed me that I forgot to ask Ray Rogers whether McCrone had returned the slides. The rest of the sessions flew by.

On Sunday, the last day of the meeting, I left early on the red-eye flight to New York, since I had a Monday morning conference. As the plane carried me through the night, I replayed the conference in my mind. Everything that I had heard, except McCrone's presentation, seemed to point to the conclusion that the images of the man in the Shroud were probably not paintings. Considering McCrone's substantial reputation, and considering his long experience as a particle expert, his pronouncement that the images were paintings carried a great deal of weight.

I wondered whether it was possible that a forger had used such a small amount of iron oxide for the images that the X-ray fluorescence could not detect it from the overall background of iron in the Shroud linen. But if the amount of iron oxide in the images was so small that X rays had not detected it, how could it be visible to the naked eye? And what about the blood on the Shroud? I was pretty sure that those seven microfibrils and the piece of biltong were blood, but I would never make a claim based on what I saw under a microscope unless I had physical and/or chemical corroboration. McCrone might be able to do it, but I wasn't willing to.

Since it didn't look as if I was going to receive more test material to work with, I reckoned that I needed to devise a definitive test for what I had. Given the contradictions between McCrone's findings and everyone else's data, the key experiment now was going to be to discover what was on my seven microfibers — red paint or blood.

Then another thought hit me. Could a medieval artist have used actual blood to depict wounds or bleeding in art? I did not believe so. Artists always sought permanent colors, and blood was not long-lasting. Would he have mixed it with something?

The next morning, before my conference, I called several professors of art history at Yale and Harvard. Did they know of any artist, fourteenth century or earlier, who used blood to paint blood? The answer was uniformly negative.

I could not discount the team members' findings. As scientists, they were too good and too meticulous for me to doubt them. Furthermore — and this was most important — their results were consistent with one another in that they all seemed to rule out an artist. But I could not undervalue McCrone's renowned expertise.

At the moment, as far as I was concerned, if the "blood" turned out to be red paint, that would solve the problem. However, if it really was blood . . . ! I did not permit myself to speculate further.

Adler and I had gotten somewhere with porphyrin chemistry. We now discussed abandoning the chemical approach for the present and turning to physics. We could try to obtain a spectrum from a garnet-red fiber and the biltong. To do so, we would have to use a microspectrophotometer, an expensive device. The instrument was very popular about twenty years ago, but better analytical methods had come along, and the usefulness of the microspectrophotometer had dwindled greatly. For uses such as measuring nucleic acids in a living cell, however, it was still an excellent tool. Another use had just cropped up — measuring blood on Shroud microfibrils. I would just have to find a microspectrophotometer somewhere and do some spectral studies. After three days, I had not located one. I decided to call Dr. George McCorkle, a classmate, who might locate one for me. He was in his laboratory in the biology department at Yale. I told him I needed to borrow a microspectrophotometer.

He asked, "What in the world do you need an instrument like that for?"

"I want to see if I can identify about seven hundred picograms of blood."

"Did you say picograms?"

"Yup."

"Why?"

I told him the whole story.

McCorkle took a long breath. "Heller, the reason I like talking with you is that we never have a normal conversation. It's always some kind of outrageous subject that has just large enough a scintilla of reason so that I don't run screaming from the room. And then, just to confound me, some of your batty ideas have a peculiar way of working out."

"I love you too, George. Now how about the microspectrophotometer?"

"I'll check it out."

The following week, McCorkle called and told me he had found one. "It belongs to Professor Joe Gall, right here in Biology. I told him why you wanted it, and he's willing, though a bit incredulous."

"I don't blame him. Aren't we all? When and where?"

We made a date, and I went to Yale with my slides. I showed them to Dr. Gall, saying, "We're going to have to take the spectrum through glass, stickum, any miscellaneous dirt on the surface of the fibrils, the garnet-red stuff, and the linen fibril itself, not to mention the Mylar."

"Well," said Gall ruefully, "I expected less than ideal conditions, but this is a mess. I don't see how you're going to see any fine structure through all that goop."

"Fine structure" refers to all the little peaks and valleys that make up the total "fingerprint" of a molecule when its spectrum is plotted graphically.

"I agree. But a couple of team members took reflectance spectra of the blood, and we can try to convert those into a transmission spectrum. Maybe we'll pick up fine structure there."

Gall shook his head after he had placed the slide under the microscope.

"Do you honestly think this is blood? This is a real clutter."

"Look," I proposed, "if this chunk, which I've named biltong, is a crystal of denatured hemoglobin, we can start with it. At least here we don't have a fiber in the way. We may be able to see the Soret band."

"The Soret band?"

"Yes. The very strong absorption due to the heme porphyrin at about four hundred and ten nanometers."

Gall replied, "Oh, yes. I recall now. But how specific is the Soret band absorption?"

"It's specific. There's nothing in nature which absorbs light at four hundred and ten nanometers that strongly. The porphyrins have an extinction coefficient of about two hundred and fifty thousand in the Soret band, which should give a peak that looks like Mount Everest."

Gall foresaw a major problem. The ultraviolet light might not be able to pass through all the interference caused by the glass, adhesive, and Mylar. If we began at the red at about 700 nanometers, and descended toward the violet, we might be able to see the beginning of a peak at 450 nanometers, but the spectrum might just go completely dark at 400 nanometers, and the curve we obtained would not mean a damn thing.

Gall and I walked around a circular corridor and went through a locked door into a small laboratory used primarily for the Zeiss microspectrophotometer. Flipping on switch after switch, Gall asked, "Incidentally, can you write in the dark?"

"I guess so. Why?"

"The room will have to be blacked out to prevent any stray light from ruining the detector's accuracy."

As the machine warmed up, Gall began to calibrate the instrument.

"I can focus down to a spot on the microscope slide about five microns [one micron equals a millionth of a meter], and we can run a spectrum there. I'll begin at seven hundred nanometers, and we will go down wavelength ten nanometers at a time. These neon numbers on this read-out are what you'll have to write down. Then we can plot them against wavelength and see what we've got."

The biltong was located, with the analytical spot right in the middle.

"Here we go," said Gall. "But these are really lousy conditions. I can't use oil, and all that other stuff is in the light path. Oh, well."

We began our readings of the biltong spot at 700 nanometers. I wrote in the dark. After each reading, we moved down 10 nanometers on the scale. There were some increases and decreases, but until these were plotted, there would be no way of knowing which part of the fingerprint of what molecule it might be.

When we reached 450 nanometers, my pulse rate began to go up. Very unscientific. At 430 nanometers, we shortened the gap between readings to 5 nanometers. At 425, the peak was still climbing. At 420 and 415, it still was rising. The crucial reading was 410. If the graph peaked here and began to fall away, we were on to something big. If, however, it continued to rise, the experiment had fallen through and was useless. At 405, there seemed to be a flattening-out. My pulse was racing.

"Calm down," I said to myself. "This is an experiment — nothing more, nothing less. The data are the data!"

When we hit 400, the peak began to fall. At 395 — more so. At 390, it was sharply down.

"Oh, my God," I said aloud, "it really is blood!"

The hair stood up on the nape of my neck. Exhilaration shot through me. This was *blood,* not iron oxide. I let out my breath with a huge whoosh, and Gall turned to me and smiled. "I guess we did it, John. Now, let's try a fibril."

The whole procedure was repeated on a garnet-red, coated microfibril. Again the Soret band appeared.

Gall had to leave for an appointment. I put the slide back in its container, placed it in my pocket, floated out to my car, and took off.

"It's blood!" ran the refrain through my head. This is a project, not a boondoggle. It is an abso-bloody-lutely first-class, interesting project. My veins felt too full.

As soon as I got to the institute, I ran in and grabbed Adler.

"Get some graph paper," I said, grinning. "We've got some plotting to do."

While I read off the coordinates I had written in the dark, Adler plotted the curves. "John," he said, "this is hemoglobin. It's the acid methemoglobin form, and it's denatured and very old."

I beamed.

"But Al," I pointed out. "We don't have the requisite fine structure."

"Fine structure, my foot! Do you think this is the spectrum of sautéed artichoke hearts? Don't be ridiculous."

"Okay. Let's check with at least two other top hemoglobin hotshots and see if they are as sure as we are. Pick anyone you want."

Adler got on the phone right away and read the coordinates to his chosen specialist. The answer — old acid methemoglobin.

Then we called Bruce Cameron on a speaker-phone. Cameron, whose double-doctorate is dedicated to hemoglobin in all its many forms, said, after we had given him the numbers and had plotted them, "You both should know what it is. It's old acid methemoglobin. I don't know why you wanted to bother me with something you know as well as I do . . . Hey, wait a minute. Are you two idiots working on the Shroud of Turin?"

Adler and I smiled at each other and shook hands. Now we were ready to tell the team.

10

Chemical Conundrums at Colorado Springs

SIX MONTHS after the Santa Barbara meeting, another weekend conclave was held, this time at Los Alamos. I could not attend, but I was sent an audiotape of the proceedings.

McCrone had gone further with his iron-oxide claims. He stated that the iron oxide was extremely finely ground, most of the particles being less than one micron in size. He then made the curious statement that submicron particles of iron oxide had not existed before 1800. It was at that time, he explained, that the process of grinding iron oxide into submicron particles was perfected. The resulting substance was known as jeweler's rouge, and was — and is — used in the fine-polishing of glass and gems. McCrone stated that there may possibly have been very faint, pre-existing images that someone had "touched up" after 1800 with an iron oxide–gelatin paint to make them more visible.

I was astonished. John Jackson called just after I had listened to the McCrone tape.

"John," Jackson queried, "have you heard the McCrone presentation?"

"Yup."

"What do you think of it?"

I told him that there had been submicron particles of iron

oxide floating around almost since the dawn of time. Its sources ranged from micrometeorites to erosion to volcanic eruptions. Besides which, the Shroud had been under lock and key ever since it came to Turin, four hundred years ago. To suggest that someone sneaked it out and repainted it *after 1800* is to claim a gigantic collusion on the part of the royal House of Savoy and the Catholic Church. Further, there exist dozens of paintings of the Shroud done before 1800, and they all look like the post–1800 paintings and photographs.

Jackson asked for up-to-date documentation. I called colleagues at various universities and government laboratories and then drafted a letter to Jackson. In it I outlined my sources: scientists at MIT, NASA, Langley Air Force Base, the Smithsonian Astrophysical Observatory, the National Center for Atmospheric Research, the University of Maryland, Michigan Tech, and Dartmouth. I listed their names and launched into a long and detailed review of all the natural sources of submicron particles of atmospheric and terrestrial iron oxide. Then I added that when the first smith hit the first piece of red-hot iron, the man-made contribution of such particles began, and it has never ceased. All of this had nothing to do with the Shroud, but I didn't believe that jeweler's rouge did either.

After receiving my letter, Jackson and Jumper decided to see if together they could make sense out of the findings to date. Except for a paper that Adler and I had published in *Applied Optics*, "Blood on the Shroud of Turin," the only record of chemical analyses done on the Shroud was McCrone's two talks, at Santa Barbara and Los Alamos. All the rest of the findings were in the realm of physics, and added up to the following results:

X-ray fluorescence

The Shroud contains the elements calcium and strontium, evenly distributed all over the cloth. Iron is also present, and is evenly distributed except in the bloodstained areas, where it is found in heavier concentrations.

What could be made of these findings? No one knew. More iron in the bloodstains made sense, since there is iron in hemoglobin. Was there iron oxide in a gelatin vehicle? What about the rest of the iron and the calcium and strontium? There were no answers at this time.

X radiographs of the Shroud

Linen would be invisible to the kind of X rays most commonly used. However, by using extremely soft X rays and sensitive techniques, we had gotten a complete set of pictures, which made the Shroud appear as though it were being held up to a very bright light. The individual threads, the warp and weft, the herringbone pattern, the burn holes and patches, could all be clearly seen.

When McCrone claimed that the images were the result of iron oxide, the radiographers immediately looked at their X rays again. Iron is very dense compared with linen, and it should have stood out in the radiographs. If the images comprised iron oxide, it should have been clearly visible in these pictures. It was not. Could there possibly be too little to be seen on the radiographs, yet enough to be seen with the naked eye, as McCrone claimed? No one thought so, but we could not be sure. What else did these pictures show? There was nothing obvious. Later, Adler and I would discover something that sent people scuttling back to look at the radiographs again. No further information had been gained from the soft X-ray photos at this time.

Image enhancement

There was no evidence of directionality or of brush strokes in the images. Additionally, there was an apparent wound in the flank.

3-D effect (computer readable)

Various artists had attempted, with no success, to reproduce the Shroud images as they appear to the unaided eye or with the aid of the VP-8. Each artistic rendering placed in the VP-8 gave a distorted, grotesque result. A reasonable statue could be made from the VP-8 information when the data of the Shroud-body distance were encoded. There was no other obvious information.

Infrared photography

The Shroud was not a conventional oil painting or a conventional water color painting; if it were, thermography would have revealed it. There was no other obvious information.

Ultraviolet and visible reflectance spectroscopy

Other than the reflectance data, which supported our transmission spectra indicating blood, there was no further information to be derived at this time.

Direct observation with
hand-held magnifying glasses and macroscopy

Low magnification, or 30 X to 40 X microscopy, will henceforth be referred to as macroscopy; microscopy means 100 X to 2000 X. (Above this magnification, electron microscopy and scanning-electron microscopy were used, giving magnifications up to and beyond 100,000 X.)

The use of hand-held magnifiers, macroscopy, and photomacroscopy showed that the images resulted from a straw-yellow color on the crowns of the threads only. There was no sign of capillary action, which ruled out liquids, or of diffusion, which ruled out vapors. Only on the crowns of the fibrils was there the straw-yellow color. There was no obvious difference in the shade of the yellow. It was merely the number of fibrils colored that determined the intensity of the images. And it was because of this *numerical* encoding of color that the VP-8 was able to read the 3-D aspect of the front and back images of the man in the Shroud. Whenever one fiber crossed another, the yellow was cut off, and the fiber beneath was white. In much of the bloodstain areas, what appeared to be blood had been abraded off the crowns of the threads and had fallen into the interstices of the weave.

There was dirt on the sole of the foot, and minute abrasions with blood and some dirt on the tip of the nose and on one knee. It was as though the man had fallen, unable to break the fall with his hands, and partly skinned his knee and nose. There seemed to be a wound in the side.

Visible and ultraviolet photography

The white-light photographs were of the highest scientific quality, revealing details never before recorded. However, the ultraviolet photography was even more informative. Evidence of lesions, abrasions, and scratches that were otherwise invisible had been found by this means. There were fluorescent haloes around some of the heavy blood flow areas and along the sides of the scourge marks. The non-image parts of the linen had a greenish-yellow fluorescence, but the image area was not fluorescent. The blood and scourge marks were black, completely absorbing the ultraviolet light. Blood has an enormous extinction coefficient because of porphyrins. In the blood areas, there *was* capillary action and the matting and adhesion typically seen when blood spills on linen.

Jackson and Jumper, initially, had two major questions:
  1. What were the images and the blood marks on the Shroud made of?
  2. How was the Shroud made?

The work that Adler and I had done indicated that the red color was indeed blood. Our work demonstrated that the microfibers and the piece of biltong were old blood. However, they came from an off-image area. Could someone with a bloody nose have touched the Shroud in the distant past? Were *all* the blood marks really blood?

None of the physical research gave any indication of what made the images or how they were made. Such data as there were seemed to diminish the possibility of the Shroud being a painting. There was no explanation for the presence of calcium, strontium, and iron in the Shroud.

Nobody except McCrone had any idea of how the images had been made.

Jumper and Jackson realized that until they understood the chemistry of this Shroud, they would simply be spinning their wheels. They called a special conference, at the Air Force Academy in Colorado Springs, and scheduled it during the spring break.

The focus would be on chemistry. Those chemically oriented would be Ray Rogers, his associate, Joan Janney, Walter McCrone, and Al Adler, whom the team had not yet met. Those dealing with physics were Jackson, Jumper, Ercoline, Pellicori, and Schwalbe. William Ercoline was a physical scientist on the faculty at the Air Force Academy. Pellicori and Schwalbe had worked on elemental analysis and spectroscopy. I was a hybrid. Vern Miller was also invited, since his scientific photography at different wavelengths, particularly in the ultraviolet, had chemical significance. Everyone agreed to come. McCrone's schedule made that week inconvenient for him, so we all changed our plans and arranged to meet the following week instead.

Jumper told McCrone that he would make available laboratories, screens, slide projectors — anything that was needed. Then, as professional scientists, we could discuss our findings and resolve our differences or agree as to where, how, and why we disagreed.

Wasn't that the way to do it? Face to face? And not in the press? Wasn't that the way that the scientific process flourished best? McCrone agreed with Jumper and was prepared to come. Jumper asked McCrone if he thought the Shroud was a fake. Absolutely, a complete fake. Did McCrone still stick to the idea of jeweler's rouge and an 1800 date? Well, came the reply, maybe he should not have said jeweler's rouge, but it was iron oxide, and all the rest was correct. Finally, McCrone added, he had arrived at a definite date when the forgery was done — 1350. He now had some new data; we could forget about the finger painting. He claimed that he had discovered the presence of a vehicle in which the iron oxide was suspended. This vehicle was a water solution of animal (collagen) gelatin. The presence of this protein was, he said, proof that the Shroud had been made with red paint.

When Adler and I arrived at the motel in Colorado Springs, Adler had to be introduced to the team. Al seems somewhat overwhelming to strangers. In the fall he lets all his hair from the neck up grow wildly. In the spring he shaves off everything except his eyebrows. I think I remember him with a tie once — at a funeral. His shirt often — and his undershirt always — has blazoned on it a huge chemical structure of the basic porphyrin molecule. He is exuberant and unflappable, a compulsive talker who has the disconcerting habit of declaiming even when he is actually listening. He has the subtlety of a tank, but he is nonetheless extremely kind and will make great personal sacrifices to help people in trouble.

When Jumper came in, he announced that he had just received a message from McCrone: he was unable to attend because of a conflict. We were genuinely sorry, because McCrone had become more of a mystery as time went on.

Very early the next morning, the whole group made its way to the Air Force Academy. The service school is magnificently surrounded by the soaring, snow-girt peaks of the Rocky Mountains. As one drives up, one sees a huge inscription on a building: BRING ME MEN! I am sure some general, whose name I should probably know, was the source of this imperative, but it and the vast buildings are dwarfed by the craggy scenery.

We entered the main building and were guided through a maze of corridors into two enormous conference rooms. Each contained a massive conference table surrounded by chairs. On one long wall, there was the mandatory tool needed for scientifc conferences — a blackboard. As certain people cannot speak without waving their hands, we seem almost tongue-tied unless we can scribble equations, structures, formulas, and the like. Laid out in neat piles were all reprints thus far published by the group. Someone had provided a microdensitometer set-up. We had projectors, screens, everything that a peculiar assortment of investigators from dissimilar backgrounds could want for a four- or five-day conference. I sat down with a satisfied grunt.

Jackson and Jumper presented their appraisal of the status of research on the Shroud. When they finished with their précis, Sam Pellicori said that as far as he was concerned, McCrone's hypothesis about iron oxide being the source of the images was just wrong. He had done a simple and elegant little experiment. He had taken some filter paper, which is white and flat, and placed on it an amount of iron oxide in the concentration that McCrone claimed existed in the images on the Shroud. Using a reflectance spectrum the Gilberts had obtained from the bloodstains on the Shroud, he had compared it to the iron oxide. The spectra did not match.

Larry Schwalbe had done something similar. He had put iron oxide into a watery solution, shaken it, and let the larger and heavier particles precipitate out. He took the suspended particles and determined the limit of resolution of the specific X-ray fluorescence equipment that was used in Turin. The minimum amount of iron oxide that could be seen by the human eye was the same amount that could be accurately determined by X-ray fluorescence. Clearly, it would be absurd for an artist to use a pigment in an amount so dilute that one could not see it with the naked eye; that was tantamount to painting in invisible ink. Schwalbe used jeweler's rouge simply because it was a convenient form of iron oxide, but he also tested other forms of the compound, and came up with the same results.

Eric Jumper said he had heard that if the iron-oxide hypothesis didn't pan out, McCrone planned to say that a good part of the color came from aged protein. Eric's G-2 has always been uncannily accurate.

After a while, irrepressible Adler said, "I don't see how we can have a meeting on chemistry when no one but McCrone has made any chemical determinations other than ours, where we claimed there was blood. Why don't we do some chemistry?"

This was a rhetorical question, but it turned on our Pied Piper. "Gosh, you guys, we have laboratories right here at the academy and microscopes and Ray has the slides back . . ."

"What!" I yelped. "We have slides?"

"Oh, sure. Didn't I tell you? Eric, Ray, and I made a special trip to Chicago to McCrone's lab to get them back."

I was positively salivating.

"John Jackson," interrupted Adler, "we can't do chemistry in your laboratories because the Air Force could not conceivably have the specialized biochemical and clinical reagents that we need."

"Try us," begged Jackson.

So Adler, Rogers, and I began to rattle off names: Schiff reagent, Biuret, Lowry's, orcinol, resorcinol, phosphomolybdate, toluene, dithizone, diphenylcarbazone . . .

Jackson, Jumper, Schwalbe, Pellicori, and Ercoline were physicists to whom the biochemical world was mysterious and unknown. Jumper and Jackson began frantically writing down the names of the requisite reagents.

"Wait," called Eric, scribbling along with Jackson. "Spell a few of those jawbreakers." We began, but Adler interrupted. "No one can remember all the details of all the tests, and, besides, we need some texts and journals that you can't possibly have . . ."

"Try us," said Jackson again.

Adler began, "Feigl, the Winchells . . ."

"Spell!" ordered Eric.

We were searching our memories, spelling reactants, equipment, and books, when something startling began to happen. Perhaps it had been prearranged, but it was as though someone had pushed a magic button: Air Force captains and majors began coming through doors. After writing down two or three names, Jumper or Jackson would tear off the paper and give it to one of the officers, who would take it and exit hurriedly. The sequence of action kept being repeated.

I thought, "Here comes one of these crazy coincidences again. The Air Force Academy is on vacation, so where are all these guys coming from? I'm not going to believe it even if it happens, but if they start returning with these items, which have to be real exotics for an undergraduate military engineering school, I'm going to start believing in the tooth fairy."

Sure enough, Air Force personnel were returning with the chemicals, equipment, and publications we needed.

The Air Force people, all of whom were on leave, were extremely eager to help. They scoured Colorado Springs for our reagents. When I asked, for example, for xylene, I was thinking of a few ounces — but suddenly a couple of officers appeared rolling a fifty-five-gallon drum of the stuff! Finally convinced that we could accomplish something, we told Jackson to lead us to the laboratory.

We set off down endless halls at a fast clip. We sea-level dwellers were breathing a bit hard in the seven-thousand-foot altitude. Then we came to a totally internal room: no windows — only walls, lined with benches, cabinets, and microscopes. Jumper pointed to one of the microscopes — a brand-new, top-of-the-line Zeiss.

Eric said, "I have one of the slides from a blood area under there. It's top-lit." (That kind of lighting is a reflective mode.)

I pounced on the microscope. "Wow!" I exclaimed. "We've got a whole jungle of stuff here. Good grief, there are microacres of what looks like blood."

"Move over," rasped Adler.

He looked. "If that isn't blood, I'll eat this microscope."

I asked Eric for a slide with body image fibers on it. He gave it to me. Adler moved over and I adjusted the microscope. The image fibers were distinct and straw-yellow compared with the nonimage fibers on the same slide. There was no question in my mind that the color of these microfibers had been caused by some yellowing agent that had no relationship to iron oxide. But could the color be the result of old gelatin? Jackson had received a letter from McCrone in which he said he had proved the presence of gelatin as a vehicle by using a color reagent called Amido black. I thought this choice of a testing agent was a poor one. We all decided, as a first priority, to test the image fibers for protein.

We worked out a production line. I would be at the big microscope, scanning the slides, picking out what was desired for testing. Vern Miller would photograph it. It would be marked and passed to Joan Janney, who sat at a macroscope with dissecting equipment. She would take out a thread and pass it to Adler, who sat before another top-lit macroscope. In front of him were bottles full of reagents, glassware, more dissecting tools, blank microscope slides, cover slips, and the like.

Before coming to Colorado Springs, Joan Janney had been playing a bit with samples of blank tape controls and the adhesive. She had put a fresh piece of tape against her blouse or sweater and then pulled off the tape and plucked the individual fibers from it. She found what I had found on the minute samples that I had. That thrice-damned adhesive was incredibly sticky. If one pulled a fiber off the surface with a forceps, the stickum would stretch out about a centimeter (half an inch) before it would snap in two — one half ricocheting back to the tape, and the other half going with the fiber, forming an instant ball of adhesive around it. Trying to pull the fiber out of the goop and away from the forceps was like trying to throw flypaper away with bare hands. It didn't work. The stickum had to be dissolved with a solvent. At the academy, xylene was the first solvent they came up with. But it took a lot of xylene to dissolve the adhesive. It made more sense to cut out the tape and dissolve the adhesive, but Joan had worked with it her way, and we had not, so we proceeded with the technique she had used.

We decided that our first test was to see whether we could confirm McCrone's assertion that gelatin was present in the images. Gelatin is a protein. We could use a test for protein that was far more sensitive than the Amido black test McCrone had used — the Biuret-Lowry. Modern photographic gelatin does not have a phenylalanine, which is necessary for a good test. However, gelatin from medieval times or earlier periods, made from hooves, horns, hides, and bones, always contained a goodly amount of it, so the test would be quite sensitive.

I would identify a fiber. Joan would pull it free, and more often than not it would fragment, because of the mechanical stress placed on it. Because of oxidation, any fabric many centuries old is somewhat fragile. Although the Shroud fibers in general were quite strong, considering the age of the linen, the fibers of the images were friable. When Adler finally received a fiber plus the adhesive blob, he would try to hold the fiber down with a needle and flush the xylene past it. When, with great patience, he isolated an intact image fibril, he added a drop of the Biuret reagent from a Pasteur pipette. He waited a minute and said, "No reaction. I call it negative. John, come take a look."

I did and said, "Confirm. Negative Biuret."

Next, he added the Lowry reagent, which increases sensitivity by a factor of ten to a hundred.

Again the result was negative.

Jackson asked to see what a positive protein test with the Biuret-Lowry looked like.

The day before, Jumper had obtained some plasma and some whole blood from the local blood bank. He had placed a drop of each on some of Maria's Spanish linen. Adler took the linen and teased out a microfibril from the plasma-drop area. He added the Biuret and immediately followed it with the Lowry. He backed off and let everyone look in the scope. There were "Oh"'s and "Ah"'s from the physicists. The thread had turned bright purple.

Then Jackson asked, "Al, can you show us that fluorescent test for porphyrin?"

Since porphyrins are Adler's favorite subject, he was delighted to oblige. He took a tiny sample of the blood from the Spanish linen, added hydrazine, and then formic acid. Dense fumes began to rise. It is a little frightening to the nonchemist the first time he sees it, because he is not expecting it. Adler loves to produce such effects on people. He called for an ultraviolet lamp, put it on, and asked that the lights be turned out. Again there were "Oh"'s and "Ah"'s from the physicists.

After the lights were turned on, Adler asked me for a Shroud fibril covered with what we both believed to be blood. I picked one that had a huge amount of red coating compared to the 700-picogram amount we had had before. He put on the reagents. Out went the lights. On went the ultraviolet. The red fluorescence could be seen with the naked eye.

"Great," cheered Larry Schwalbe.

"Neat," said Jackson.

"First rate," exclaimed Miller.

With the new slides in hand, we had tested a blood area directly — and it was indeed blood. We had tested an image area for gelatin with a better test than Amido black, and we found none. Of course, if the Shroud turned out not to be a painted object, the problem became much more complex. Obviously, the images had been made by something, and some other form of human, artistic enterprise was next on our list of hypotheses. Chemical reaction with a human corpse would be tested subsequently as a possible cause of the images.

All of us were excited by these preliminary findings. But that is all they were — preliminary.

As all the members returned to their chores, we decided to do some controls to see how sensitive the Biuret-Lowry is for gelatin. Adler told the physicists to make a 10 percent gelatin solution, then 5 percent, 2.5 percent, 1 percent, and 0.5 percent. They bustled about. Vern Miller took some of the 10 percent solution and the ultraviolet light, and disappeared into another lab. About two minutes later, he popped in and said, "Hey, you guys, the gelatin fluoresces like crazy! We don't have to do all that chemistry to prove that there's no protein in the image fibers. We already know that the images aren't fluorescent, so there can't be any gelatin there."

I explained that if the lab gelatin they had just made up for standards was pure, that is, photographic grade, it would not contain any significant amounts of the three amino acids responsible for the fluorescence. These were tyrosine, phenylalanine, and tryptophan. The physicists immediately wanted to get some film-grade gelatin for standards. I told them not to bother, for people in medieval times would have boiled up horns, hooves, hides, or bones, and would not have known or cared whether the three fluors were present.

Bill Butler, a professor of chemistry at the Air Force Academy, interjected, "You did say skin and bones are the source of gelatin?"

I nodded, and he asked, "How about rat tails?"

Weirdest question I had heard in a month. I shook my head. "What, which, I mean — rat tails?"

"If we boiled up some rat tails, wouldn't we get gelatin?"

"Sure, but if they're fresh, you're going to get a lot of other stuff with it, including denatured proteins and . . ."

"How about frozen rat tails?"

This conversation was rapidly losing me. "How in the name of all that is slightly rational does one go about finding frozen rat tails?"

"I have some."

I had gone into that lab to try to do some chemistry, and now I was beginning to think I had begun to lose my hold on reality. I murmured, "You just happen to have some frozen rat tails. Are they in your attic? In a trunk, maybe?"

Butler ignored me and said, "Tails are mostly skin and bones, aren't they?"

"Uh-huh," I replied.

He left. I turned back to the microscope.

Ten minutes later, when I looked around, I saw a beaker full of rat tails and water, boiling merrily on a hot plate. The concoction smelled like chicken soup. I decided to pretend I hadn't seen it and tried to concentrate on what I saw through the microscope. I thought to myself that scientists don't just become absent-minded professors — they are driven to it. Shortly after, some Air Force majors peered through the doorway, and one asked me what smelled so good. I told him that he really did not want to know.

Adler then determined that he could easily obtain a positive protein test on a fibril that had a 0.5 percent gelatin coating on it, either with the standard that was in the laboratory or with the rat-tail variety. Further dilution would be gilding the lily. Gelatin in a 0.5 percent aqueous solution is little better than pure water as a suspending agent for a heavy pigment like iron oxide. In addition, Vern Miller and Sam Pellicori found that they could detect the 0.5 percent rat-tail gelatin by its fluorescence. From somewhere in the academy, some of the ever-helpful Air Force officers had located some centuries-old volumes with original bindings. The glue for the spines had been made from hooves, bones, and horns; today, some European leatherworkers still use such glue. Miller exposed the books to ultraviolet light and gleefully reported that the backings of these Renaissance volumes fluoresced. We knew from the experiments in Turin that the images did not. Except for myself, everyone was convinced that there was no protein in the images, as opposed to the blood areas, on the Shroud. I held out until I could repeat the whole process under more rigorous conditions, with even more sensitive tests, again and again.

Meanwhile I had been examining the slides we had gotten back from McCrone. Many had had chunks excised, and ink from the felt-tip pens he had used had seeped under the Mylar backing of the adhesive strips. There was one heck of a lot of debris present, both modern and ancient. I found a colorful array of natural and synthetic fibers — among them, linen of different shades, tints, and degrees of corrosion, cotton, silk, wool, animal hairs, modern synthetic fibers of different types and colors, insect parts, tiny droplets of what appeared to be beeswax from church candles, modern fly ash, crystals, particulates of different sizes and shapes, dust, spores, pollens, and much material I could not identify without more study. What made everything more difficult was that when McCrone had pressed the tape onto the glass slides, air pockets had been entrapped, and in some areas the adhesive was beginning to crystallize. All in all, unsnarling this was going to take a great deal of work.

I recalled that these pieces of Mylar tape had been put on the Shroud with a relatively few grams of pressure. The first material that would have adhered to the adhesive would be the most recent surface debris. The next would be a random sampling of the next layer, and so on. However, hard compression of the Mylar onto glass slides had squeezed everything together. Furthermore, repeated folding of the Shroud over the years had caused transposition of substances from one area to another. We would never see a "pure" picture.

The fibrils from the images continued to be negative for

protein, and the bloodstain ones continued to be positive for blood. Then we tested a bloodstain area for protein, and it was positive — as one would expect of real blood. Blood is loaded with different types of protein, such as albumins and globulins. Night fell, and some Air Force officers brought in sandwiches. Without pause, we ate and kept repeating the tests till after midnight.

The following day, Adler and I were still doing tests. Everyone was extremely impatient to find out whether McCrone was right or wrong. If it was determined that his claims did not hold up on a preliminary basis, then the others would be willing to go on to other questions. The next thing on our agenda was to find out if iron oxide was present on image fibers. X-ray fluorescence had found none, X radiographs had seen none, and Pellicori's iron-oxide spectrum was significantly different from the Gilberts' spectrum of the actual Shroud images. At the Santa Barbara meeting, when Jackson had asked McCrone how he explained the fact that X-ray fluorescence had seen no iron increase in an image area, McCrone had dismissed the issue by stating that the X-ray data must have been in error or were not sensitive enough.

That morning, Jumper announced that he had been looking at slides and that in at least a third of the image fibrils, there were no red particles at all.

"How," he demanded, "could iron-oxide pigment be the cause of the images if it's not present in at least thirty-three percent of the image fibers?"

Others in the group checked his observations and confirmed them.

I had been looking at the red dots and blobs on image and nonimage fibrils, and, increasingly, they looked like blood. I said so. Immediately, we began to collect individual fibrils with red dots. One by one they were placed on the slide. Now that we had a definitive test for blood in the blood areas, the determination as to whether all the red dots were blood or iron-oxide particles would be relatively easy.

Janney, Jackson, Jumper, and Pellicori wanted to know what was going to happen. Adler explained, "I'm about to add hydrazine. If the red particle goes into solution, it's got to be blood protein. It can't be iron oxide."

Jumper asked why iron oxide would not dissolve in hydrazine.

I asked him, "If you placed a horseshoe in a bowl of water, would it dissolve in five minutes?"

"Of course not!"

"That's your answer. Iron has a very low solubility."

Adler added the hydrazine, and the red particles began dissolving.

"And," crowed Al, "they're producing the typical hemochromagen color. This, lady and gentlemen, is *not* iron oxide; it is blood!"

For the next few days, repeated tests for protein in image fibers were negative. The red particles dissolved in hydrazine. There was, of course, protein in the bloodstain areas but not in the body image areas. Other tests were done, but by now we had enough unequivocal data to serve as a solid base for a preliminary conclusion that the images were not gelatin and iron oxide and that the blood was in fact blood. We had not ruled out unconventional colors and other methods of image making, but McCrone's hypothesis was unlikely.

Ruling things out is the next best procedure to ruling things in. It's not quite as exciting, but when it is pushed to its ultimate, whatever is left is usually going to be the right answer.

As we prepared to leave, Jackson asked me whether Yale still had the Vinland map.

"Sure. Why?"

"Eric and I were thinking. Since McCrone proclaimed it a fake, it can't be worth much. Maybe we can buy it from Yale for a few thousand dollars."

11

Textile Technology, Painters,
Pigments, Fibrils, and
the Debris of Ages

ADLER AND I made the plane at the Colorado Springs Airport — but barely. I took a deep breath as the aircraft took off. We had the slides. That meant that we were now the donkey, and the team had pinned the tail on us.

We both sat back and pondered the days ahead.

It seemed increasingly clear to me that the chemical problems posed by the dirt, debris, fibers, and particles on those glass microscope slides held the answers to the whole Shroud problem. All of the physics experiments performed by other team members had posed more questions than they had answered. The two initial questions that had been raised before the team went to Turin remained unanswered:

1. What were the images and blood marks?
2. How was the Shroud made?

McCrone had the answers. He claimed it was *the* answer: the whole thing, including the blood, was a painting made by a human hand. He had over two decades of experience with this kind of problem and a worldwide reputation. Adler and I, on the other hand, had never before tackled anything remotely like an artistic forgery.

At first, I had been concerned about becoming involved

with what looked like a controversial, religious relic, but I had been sufficiently intrigued to take a cautious peek. I had thought the probability that the Shroud was a painting was overwhelming. However, now there were these findings by the physicists in the group which contradicted that hypothesis. Also, we had found blood. Jackson had asked me if I thought it possible that a fourteenth-century artist might have used actual blood to paint a bloody image. When I made inquiries of several professors of art history in regard to medieval and Renaissance pigments, I had been told that artists of those times were always searching for paints and pigments that would endure. As a result, they were partial to metal salts, such as orpiment (arsenic sulfide) or litharge (lead oxide). Blood would change color and denature; on a fabric, if laid on as thickly as in the Shroud, it would abrade and flake — as, in fact, it had done. It seemed to me unlikely that anyone would have used real blood as paint. But if someone was forging a shroud, he just might have.

I asked Adler how he felt about it.

"Hey, the data are the data. McCrone can say anything he wants to. All I want him to do is publish it. Then we'll see how his data compare to ours."

That was going to be the crux of it. In science, anybody can say anything he wants to, but it is not until it is openly published in a respected scientific journal that it becomes official. There is a tough screening mechanism that is used universally by all major scientific journals. When an author submits a paper for publication, the editor sends copies to eminent scientists in the field. These scientific peers study the article closely. They evaluate whether the experimental methods and techniques are up to their own standards. The data and the conclusions are appraised, and even the bibliography is studied. The critiques of each of these peer reviewers are sent to the author, who must do whatever is required to conform to their suggestions. This may mean carrying out more experiments, trying different methods, setting up more rigorous statistical standards, and so on. The STURP group had decided, in advance, that because of the potentially controversial nature of the Shroud work, all their papers should be sent to the major journals so that the work could be critically vetted before publication.

When we went out to Colorado Springs, neither Adler nor I had any idea of becoming this involved. When we left, Jumper had put the slides in Adler's hands with the imperative "Go do chemistry," and on the long flight back east we seemed to arrive at a consensus that we would do so, without really debating the issue. The plane landed at Kennedy Airport, and we were delighted to be able to grab a limousine for Connecticut at once and catch up on our sleep.

A week passed. Every day I would spend one or two hours looking at the slides. I had set up several microscopes, equipped to examine the slides with different light sources and different optics. By the second week, I had become familiar with what all of the slides looked like, but I was not one iota more informed as to what any of them signified. As far as I was concerned, I knew positively only one thing about the Shroud. It had real blood on it.

However, there was still the other crucial problem: what had made the body images? To answer that, all we had to do was rule out every known and unknown coloring agent — paint, pigment, dye, ink, stain — that had ever been used.

Earlier, I had made some inquiries into what was known about colorants of different lands, climes, ages, empires, and schools. There are classic sources, such as D'Arcy Thompson, Vasari, and Eastlake, to mention but three of many. Also available for reference are such eminent societies as the American Association of Textile Chemists and Colorists, and the British Society of Dyers and Colourists. There is the work of many investigators specializing in organic and inorganic colorants. I was trying to identify as many known materials as possible that might produce a straw-yellow or red color so that we could begin by testing for known materials and leave the more difficult area of the unknown for our final effort.

At first one gets the impression of great knowledge and a thoroughly covered field, except that there is a vast amount not known. Many artists of yesteryear made their own colors and were often secretive about their recipes. We know of many substances that were used, and others that may have been used but later oxidized away, leaving no trace. There were artists who thought they were using a "pure" material that worked wondrously well, when, in fact, the reason it was so useful was that it contained an unknown contaminant. To make matters worse, the chemical structure of many components varies over time.

In the process of learning their trade, artists invariably took an interest in what their predecessors and contemporaries did. Fading pictures, flaking materials, changing and degrading colors, were every artist's enemy. It seems as though human nature demands one's best effort for any chance at immortality. For example, rocks have always seemed to man as among the most long-lasting things on earth. Suppose one takes a vivid, green rock, like malachite, grinds it in a metal mortar and pestle, and mixes it with a vehicle — one would have a malachite-green paint. Why should it not last for generations? In fact, it does. However, there are never enough minerals to cover the color spectrum required by art, so experimentation is required. In this, the painter of an earlier age was joined by the alchemists, who, in spite of their vain search for the philosopher's stone, accomplished some rather remarkable chemical advances. Recent and not so recent discoveries have persuaded me never to sell ancient technology short. Man has an IQ that is no higher today than it was 50,000 years ago. Our ancestors' tribes had their geniuses, even as we do. Periodically, archeology turns up an ancient artifact that is a real shocker and demonstrates that someone in the distant past was clever enough to figure out something we thought had evolved only in fairly recent times. Any argument *ex silencio* is a dangerous one. Something may never have been recorded in a historical sense, but that does not mean it was not known. This is part of the puzzle of the past, and the challenge of historical research.

There is, however, another side of formulations that has a distinctly nutty aspect, intermixed with man's penchant for mystery and secrecy. It is this aspect which must, perforce, make one cautious. The most recent experience I had had with recipes, combining mixtures of sense plus a degree of lunacy, had to do with drilling "mud" for oil wells. One recipe calls for pecan shells and another for dozens of shredded copies of the *Houston Chronicle* — Sunday edition.

For scientific purposes, all colors can be divided into two main categories, organic and inorganic, and one subcategory, metallorganic. Inorganics and metallorganics can be identified by key elements, and there are a number of extremely sensitive methods used to detect these elements. From our point of view, these techniques were too sensitive. The fibrils and particles on the tapes were at least 630 years old; perhaps 2000 years. Over the period of at least six centuries, dust, debris, pollution, and other contaminants had covered the Shroud, adding new factors.

From history we knew that untold thousands of hands, both clean and grubby, had touched and fondled it. It had been kissed by innumerable people, both clean-shaven and with beards and mustaches. We had discovered that it was not unusual for over 90 percent of the people who have access to the Shroud to touch something personal to its surface. STURP members knew of postage stamps and pictures that had touched its surface. One cleric had taken out a stained cotton kerchief and placed it on the Shroud. According to the cleric, he had kept the kerchief, unlaundered, in his pocket since he had used it to touch the Holy Sepulcher in Jerusalem years before. Untold bizarre materials must have had contact with the Shroud's surface.

If we used techniques that were too sensitive, we would

find elements representing all this clutter, from mites to dandruff that had fallen on the Shroud. We needed techniques that were just good enough to test for levels of substances the eye could see. If some substance existed below the visible level, we reasoned, it could have nothing to do with the images. The level of detection had to be of just the right order of magnitude.

Some microscopic observations could be ignored. For example, I was cataloguing all the different kinds of fibers that I saw. There was plain wool, red silk, blue linen, plain cotton, green polyester — and all of a sudden I came on a pink thread. It was a synthetic, because I could see certain linear scoring along the side, typical of synthetic production. I called Adler over. "Al, take a look at this. It looks to me like pink nylon."

He said, "It sure does. Let's test it."

We did. It was not only pink nylon, but elastic pink nylon, like the kind used in girdles and such.

"Al, in twenty-five words or less, explain to me how a pink girdle got on the Shroud."

"I shudder to think," he replied.

This was one of those wild and wonderful incongruities that occur periodically. It is the kind of thing for which one really does not want a pedestrian answer; it is too much fun to speculate.

Adler wanted to begin the tests that would include or exclude some specific common organic structures that might be present. So he proceeded to test image fibrils for phenols, riboflavin, steroids, indoles, lignin, starch, pyrroles, creatinine, urea derivatives, uric acid, and nitro derivatives. They were all negative.

"You know, Al," I needled, "I'll bet you did some of these tests just because you had the reagents handy."

In my presence, Adler had never admitted error.

"Hey," he riposted, "you never can tell."

We then set up a more formal protocol for the serious work. We set a date, and Adler arrived at the appointed hour. I told him that, first and foremost, I wanted to do a large series of controls. We could use the three-hundred-year-old Spanish linen for that purpose.

Adler inquired, "How much Spanish linen do you think you have left?"

"For control purposes, I have acres."

Whereas we constantly griped and complained about the problems and agony of having to work with nearly invisibly small samples under a microscope, there was never a problem with controls. One square centimeter (less than half an inch) provided enough control fibers for six months of work.

I told my colleague, "I have a couple of other really neat linen items for controls, in addition to Maria's Spanish sample."

"Oh?"

"I also have a sample of Coptic funerary linen from about A.D. 350 and a Pharaonic linen one of about 1500 B.C."

"Are you serious?"

"Yup."

"You constantly surprise me."

"Trust your medic."

"Sure. While you're in a providing mood, do you have a copy of Chamot and Mason or Kirk or Feigl or Shaffer or Winchell and Winchell? We'll need them." (These were all scientific texts.)

"No. Don't you?"

"I have an old Feigl and the Winchells, but I want the latest ones."

Adler has a personal library of about thirty-five thousand volumes — at least five thousand of them are scientific — and he claims he has read most of them. I have a library of about thirty thousand books, and only fifteen volumes are scientific and reference works. Adler loves old and new texts on science and technology. I do not. Neither Adler nor I have enough shelf space at home. Books are on every available flat surface, including floors, to the endless annoyance of our wives. Adler just cannot believe that I refuse to keep more than fifteen books on science at home, so he always calls if he cannot find a particular volume. Finally, he asked, "Well, if you don't have them, I guess you wouldn't happen to have an Ott, Spurlin, and Grafflin?"

"Al, you know I don't have . . . You mean all five volumes?"

"Yes. You and I are going to have to read them."

We argued about it for forty minutes. At last I agreed to borrow a set from Yale.

A few days later, still grumbling, I turned over the thick volumes to Adler. The title of this magnum opus is *Cellulose and Cellulose Derivatives*. It is *the* definitive work on the subject. Cellulose is made up of sugars. Sugars are either five carbon-atom structures (pentoses), or six carbons (hexoses). All sugars are saccharides. Polymers of sugars are polysaccharides. Cellulose is a polysaccharide. Wood, cotton, linen, and rayon are all made of cellulose or cellulose derivatives. What is not in Ott, Spurlin, and Grafflin is not worth bothering about.

Adler asked, "Which volumes will you read?"

"Listen, Al, I got them for you. You're always saying, 'Trust your chemist!' Fine! I trust you to read them. Among my many lifelong ambitions, one is not to become a polysaccharide chemist. You read them, and when you come to the juicy parts, tell me about them."

He complained, but took away the books and began reading.

Ten days later he came to see me. "I've just finished learning all about cellulose and its derivatives. It's now going to take me ten years of hard work to forget it. I've acquired more useless knowledge than I ever wanted, and it's all your fault."

I let him gripe until he ran down. Then, with a sly look on his face, he said, "What do you know about the process of retting linen?"

"Isn't that something that you do to the flax plant to get linen fibers from it?"

"Yes, but what do you know about it?"

"Nothing."

"Well, I do, and it's important. Remember, I told you to read Ott . . ."

"O.K. O.K. You found something. What?"

"Well," he started smugly, "it seems that in order to ret linen, you take the flax plant and soak it in a natural body of water, like a river or lake. The useless part of the flax kind of rots away, and the fibers that remain are linen, which is spun into thread."

"And?"

"Well, during the retting, the linen fibers act as an ion exchanger, and do you know what ions they take up selectively from water?"

"You're funning me!"

"Nope. Calcium, strontium, and iron!"

"Hallelujah! That explains the X-ray fluorescence data."

I called John Jackson right away to tell him the glad tidings. I could almost hear his grin on the phone.

"That's really neat. Really neat. Say, I wonder why McCrone didn't know that?"

I answered, "John, neither Al nor I knew it. And I'm not sure how many people besides Ott, Spurlin, and Grafflin do. You could probably put them all in a small room. Don't worry about it; revel in it. I'll let you pass on the good word to the rest of the team."

The first order of business for us was to establish controls. Fortunately, we had the Spanish linen — all we could possibly need — both with and without blood on it. Then there were the samples of Pharaonic linen, though they were very small. There were many other linens we could have obtained, but these three seemed reasonable to start with, for whatever the age of the Shroud — 630 years or 2000 years — we had it bracketed with the cloth samples on hand.

We began by designing controls that would test what
(a) we already knew,

(b) we suspected,

(c) others claimed.

What facts were inarguable? That it was old — at least six hundred years. That the patches were about five hundred years old or less. That it had been in a fire, and some of it was scorched, charred, or burned through. The temperature of the old molten silver would have been about 900°C. The temperature of the Shroud farthest from the burn holes would have reached somewhere between ambient temperature (about 22°C) and the onset of pyrolysis of linen (about 200°C). Furthermore, the burning of holes in the linen occurred in a closed metal casket, where there was probably a limited oxygen atmosphere. (There was some physical and chemical evidence of this. Vern Miller's experiment at the academy with burning linen in a limited-oxygen atmosphere had produced a furfural-type material, which fluoresced in the ultraviolet. This jibed with the ultraviolet reflectance spectra of the Shroud itself.)

We established thermal controls at several different temperatures. Since we had found blood, we would make duplicate thermal controls of fibers with blood on them. It would be my two-year-old blood on three-hundred-year-old linen, but that was as close as we could come for the present.

McCrone had claimed the existence of very finely dispersed, tiny iron-oxide particles in a gelatin-water solution. We would make a tenth of a 1 percent gelatin solution — so thin that it would be difficult to tell by the sticky-finger test that it was not plain water. Gelatin (or egg albumin or milk protein) is used as a vehicle in which particles or pigment can be suspended. If it is too dilute, it will not suspend anything. One tenth of 1 percent is so thin as to be ridiculous for a vehicle, but we knew we could easily detect protein on a fibril at that concentration. If there was none at 0.1 percent, we could probably rule out gelatin as a vehicle. However, when we went down to 0.01 percent, we could still detect protein. Into these dilute gelatin solutions, we would put 0.1 percent of jeweler's rouge, dispersing it with ultrasonics — far more thoroughly than any artist could do. This concentration of iron particles in the one-micron range would yield approximately the number of particles on a fiber that McCrone claimed was present. We would perform thermal controls on these gelatin–iron oxide samples as well.

Finally, one of Ray Rogers' collaborators, Diane Soran, suggested that the bleaching process for linen two thousand years ago might have used ashes and an extract of soapwort. Adler, whose intense and ongoing interest in scouting had made him a first-class field naturalist, knew exactly where to go to find some growing wild. It was plucked and extracted, and the linen was soaked in the extract. Thermal controls were to be repeated with these fibers. This was the initial batch of controls.

We decided to explore as complete a range of known color possibilities as we could gather. I had spent a long time delving into the matter of blood used as paint. Now I spent just as long learning all I could about paints — their sources, vehicles, uses. I talked to modern artists, artists who specialized in medieval and Renaissance colors, art historians who specialized in various periods from the fourteenth century in France, Byzantium, Florence, Venice, going backward in time to find out everything that anyone knew, guessed, or hypothesized about vehicles (including gelatin), their concentrations, sources, and uses. I asked all of them about pigments, paints, dyes, and stains. I contacted museum curators who were responsible for the restoration of art objects, paintings, hangings, and textiles of the period of A.D. 50 to A.D. 1400 of European, Byzantine, Arab, Persian, and North African provenance. I also included China, Korea, and Japan. If anyone complained because I hadn't covered Khmer, Tibetan, or Afghan sources, I would challenge them to a game of buzkashi.

Our scientific estimates of sources and ranges of concentrations of gelatins turned out to be well within known or estimated numbers. From a 1 to 10 percent concentration of gelatin made from hides, hooves, horns, or bones, from the purest to the crudest, made from boiled everything — with or without deadly anthrax bacilli, a common contaminant in some imported materials — all were used. We would measure the lowest levels of concentration to see if protein of any kind was present, with 0.1 percent as our lowest level of detection. Subsequently we would improve our detection considerably below 0.1 percent. As for the iron oxides, we used higher concentrations of a mixture of red ocher and yellow ocher, which was clearly in excess of the largest number of red particles that McCrone claimed, as well as those within his range and below it. Though we did corroborate Jumper's estimate that a minimum of a third of the image fibrils had no red particles, we sought and located image fibrils that had the most red particles and used a concentration of red and yellow iron oxides that matched the greatest of those.

One physical test that provided a means of discriminating between iron-oxide particles and blood particles was a test for birefringence. Because of the crystalline nature of iron oxide, transmitted light is split, and the appropriate optics can show this. Blood is not crystalline and does not manifest this property. The only way that someone could have been misled into thinking that the blood particles on the Shroud were birefringent is if he had examined them for this property while they were still on the Mylar tape. Mylar is optically active, and *any* red particle looks birefringent when the light has to pass through the tape and particle. The particles had to be removed from the tape if one was to determine which were blood and which were not. This rather simple observation would turn out to be an extremely critical one in ascertaining whether or not McCrone's claims were correct.

At Colorado Springs all the red particles we had looked at were blood. After we returned to our own laboratories and were able to work at a less hectic pace, we also found some iron oxide, but it was in a very sharply delineated area of the Shroud and had nothing at all to do with images and blood.

Meanwhile, I had run across a field of six linen fibrils with red particles *inside* each of them. Under a microscope, a fiber of linen looks like a stalk of bamboo. It has nodes just like bamboo, and the walls of the tube in between the nodes are relatively thick. Particles cannot penetrate those walls any more than one could get marbles through the walls of a piece of bamboo without punching holes in the stalk. In the case of linen, water molecules are small enough to penetrate the "walls," as are completely dissolved salts in solution. But blood and iron-oxide particles of the one-micron range are just too huge. How did they get inside that fibril? The nodes were intact; the structure wasn't fractured. This was as crazy as finding marbles inside an intact bamboo pole. It didn't make sense!

Working patiently, I was able to establish that the particles were absolutely and unequivocally inside the linen, and that the fibers and their nodules were intact. I waited till Adler confirmed my observations. The slide was from a water-stain area. Some of the red particles on the slide were birefringent, indicating iron oxide. The particles inside the linen also seemed to be birefringent, but the linen fiber may have distorted what we were seeing. We were stumped.

Suddenly Adler yelled, "Khaki! What do you know about khaki?"

"It was the color of our work uniforms in the Navy . . ."

"No, no, no," he interrupted. "What do you know about making khaki?"

Before I could ask him what khaki had to do with the Shroud of Turin, he ran out of the laboratory and was gone. Three days later he called and asked me to come over to his lab. Mystified, I complied. He gave me a slide and asked me to tell him what I saw. One always begins with low magnification and works up. I took one look at 50 X, and said, "It's linen."

"Marvelous," he said sarcastically. "Now look at it under higher power."

I did, and my jaw flapped. "You," I accused, "have got half a zillion red particles inside the linen fibrils. How did you pull that off?"

He grinned and said, "Khaki."

Somewhere, he had read about an old method of making khaki. We knew that water and salts dissolved in water can permeate linen fibers. The khaki makers had used a soluble iron salt, which entered into the fibers and adhered to their surface. The dyers would then precipitate iron as a hydroxide, both on and inside the fibers, with alkali, and follow up by dehydrating the cloth, which would "fix" and convert the hydroxide into iron-oxide particles within and on the fiber.

Beautiful! Of course, nobody got marbles into bamboo. They injected molten glass into it and let it harden! That is a pretty wild analogy, but apt. Now, at least, we had a mechanical way of getting the genie into the bottle. All we had to do was relate this way of making khaki with the apparently strange distribution of iron-oxide particles on the Shroud. Adler was beginning to have an inkling.

"Nice work," I said. "Now explain the rest of the iron oxide."

He froze. His eyes squinted. He shut up and I waited. When he acts this way, he is about to give birth to an idea.

"Khaki," he said. "Khaki."

"Hey. We've just gone through that exercise and . . ."

He merely harumphed. He was gestating. At least 50 percent of the time, this type of behavior produced a first-class insight. This was one of those times.

When I next saw him, two weeks later, he was wearing a smug grin. He told me that he had an explanation for the iron oxide. He had made an ingenious reconstruction of what had happened 450 years ago.

We knew that when the linen of the Shroud was retted, the fibrils had absorbed large amounts of iron. It was evenly spread over the entire surface. We had determined that this form of iron was fairly loosely bound to the cellulose in the fibrils' surface.

Adler had put together what he had learned of the old way of making khaki and what we knew of the 1532 fire. After part of the top of the casket melted, and molten drops of silver had burned through the folded cloth, the box had been doused with water. That water had reached very high temperatures and, spreading out, had carried with it iron from the fibers to the edges of the water stains. There, the iron had precipitated as iron hydroxide, and dehydration had converted it to iron oxide. The iron oxide, therefore, should all be at the water-stain margins.

In checking the slides, Adler found that this is exactly what had happened. Until this point, neither of us had considered the water-stain margins to be important, but now we knew that we could corroborate Al's findings by checking the iron content inside the water stains. If much of the iron from the fibers had been carried to the edges of the stains, then the iron content of the fabric inside the stain areas must be lower than at the margins. And that is what he found. It was a really neat piece of historical re-creation.

We then proceeded to check a huge number of red particles. Most of them tested positive for blood. The water-stain margins contained the iron oxide. Naturally, where the margins intersected other features, such as the images, there was also iron oxide present.

Then Adler said, "I'll bet you that all the red dots and globs will turn out to be blood, and the rest will be the iron oxide."

He was almost right. There would be one major exception.

12

Human Blood and — Cinnabar

ADLER AND I decided we had done enough looking at and testing of red dots and blobs. It was time to start testing fibrils in order to find out what had caused the yellow color.

At Colorado Springs we had not found protein of any kind on the body images. Back in my own labs I would use a very tiny scalpel blade to remove fibrils and would cut out the Mylar tape around each one. An extremely delicate scissors, the kind used in ophthalmic surgery to cut the iris, a microforceps, and a glass needle were my tools. A fibril is 15 microns in diameter. For comparison, a red blood cell is 7 microns in diameter. Cutting out this thin a sliver has to be done under the microscope. The scalpel blade has to be wetted with precisely the right amount of solvent. If there is not enough, the very sticky adhesive pulls like a rubber band and snaps, and one never is aware until later whether the fibril has snapped back or stayed on the excised Mylar portion. Too much solvent, and the fibril stays behind in a micropool. I wanted to begin all over, as though we had done no testing of protein at Colorado Springs. Adler concurred.

Although the Biuret-Lowry is a good test for protein, it has a limitation. We began by quantizing the sensitivity of all protein tests that might be applicable. These included the Amido black, Coomasie brilliant blue, Biuret-Lowry, ninhydrin, and fluorescamine. On control fibers, we placed known amounts of photographic-grade gelatin, ordinary gelatin, and blood proteins. With fluorescamine, we could detect protein at the one-nanogram level, the most sensitive test by a factor of ten.

Deciding to check the blood-area fibrils first, we picked a fibril from what we believed was a serum area, which should have been laden with blood proteins. (These are honey-colored compared with the straw-yellow of images, and are easily distinguishable.) I excised a fibril with its Mylar backing. The plastic-tape sliver and its adhesive had to be carefully washed away until the fibril was "clean" on the tiny dimple well of a slide. Using a one-lambda pipette (containing a thousandth of a milliliter), we filled it with fluorescamine and added it to the fibril. The lights were turned off and the ultraviolet went on, and the erstwhile honey-yellow fibril glowed with a positive test like a bright green fluorescent beacon. We repeated this again and again on one honey-yellow fibril after another from every sample that contained such fibrils. However, this test and the positive hemoglobin tests were not done in the absence of other data. They were added to other observations. When I had just put some of my whole blood on the Spanish linen, the fluid flowed under the microscope like dilute molasses. The red color oozed around the linen fibrils and did not penetrate them. Viewing under low power (40 X), I could see where the linen fibers were stuck together by the sticky blood proteins. I could also see the meniscus. The same effect could be seen in the 50 X macrophotographs taken of the blood area of the Shroud.

We then proceeded to do fluorescamine tests of image microfibrils. If they had red dots, which might be flakes of blood and hence would contain protein, we removed them first. Before we were through, we had tested several hundred of these fibrils from the various image samples. In none was there any gelatin or any other protein. Each fibril test took about forty minutes.

Under normal circumstances, these tests should have been sufficient. However, because of the nature of this entire project, sufficient was not good enough, and we decided to make the tests exhaustive. We knew we would be scrutinized hypercritically by any peer-review board, and we wanted *all* the answers.

STURP reached the same conclusions about quality and had set up its own peer-review group to criticize any paper before it was sent to a journal whose own scientific reviewers would have the last word. STURP's reviewers were uncompromisingly and painfully tough and thorough — in particular, Jumper, Schwalbe, Pellicori, Rogers, and Druzik. Jim Druzik was a new member of the team with a specialty in polysaccharide chemistry. He worked at the Los Angeles County Museum of Art. Consequently, Adler and I began a whole new set of experiments to resolve the gelatin and blood question.

We made up a solution of powerful proteolytic enzymes. Enzymes are biological molecules that make the body function. Proteolytic enzymes attack and destroy proteins. Meat tenderizers contain such enzymes. Taking control fibers, we added gelatin in various concentrations down to 0.01 percent and impregnated the fibers with it. They gave, of course, a positive protein test. We added the enzymes and waited until they had done their thing and then retested the fibers. As we expected, they were negative. We exposed the honey-coated serum-clad fibers from a bloodstain area to the enzymes, which destroyed the serum proteins, leaving a "clean" fiber that looked like the off-image fiber. Then straw-yellow image fibers were placed in the enzyme solution. They remained straw-yellow. This was simply another confirmation that there was no "aged protein" responsible for the color of the images.

While we were doing all these tedious, repetitious tests

in New England, other events were occurring in the middle of the country.

McCrone had never been a member of STURP and had nothing to do with the organization until he obtained the Mylar tapes from Ray Rogers. Jackson and Jumper asked the board of trustees of STURP to offer McCrone membership in order not to exclude someone who wished to do constructive work on the Shroud. McCrone accepted the offer. He had submitted two papers for peer review. The reviews were, as always, rigorous, and they pulled no punches. McCrone, feeling insulted, resigned. He subsequently printed his papers in his own little journal, *The Microscope*, published by his McCrone Institute. Of course, this did not meet our standards of a major peer-review journal, and I found that no university libraries in the area carried *The Microscope*. To obtain a copy of the two papers, I called Jumper, our G-2 expert, who eventually found and sent me Xerographic copies. In these two curious documents, McCrone made no mention of any of the results of the physical findings or of the presence of blood — all of which had been published in the standard scientific literature — except to dismiss them. He merely quoted his own microscopic observations and reiterated that the whole Shroud — images and bloodstains alike — was red paint. However, there was one point of enlightenment. He mentioned that he had measured the birefringence of the red particles while they were *on* the Mylar tape.

Jumper called soon afterward and asked when we would be ready to publish.

"Eric," I replied, "we're quite sure that there's no gelatin or any other protein in the images, but we have no idea what made the images or how they were created. It would be dumb if we just published a negative datum."

Jumper explained that since McCrone had made public that the Shroud was a painting, the press had been swarming and his phone had been ringing off the hook. He urged us to get cracking.

Up to now, we had been under some scientific pressure to produce data, but a new element had been introduced. It was pressure by the press. I had never run into this before. We had — as have all scientists — an obligation to the public. It is from the public, in the final analysis, that we obtain our funding, laboratories, libraries, equipment, and the like, whether the donor of scientific dollars is an individual, a foundation, a corporation, or the government. We have an obligation to expend these funds wisely and to find and report the truth. Normally, the public-at-large is only peripherally aware of scientists. It is only when there is something like a space spectacular or a biomedical breakthrough (loathsome word) that anyone outside the scientific community is aware of us.

In the case of the Shroud research, there was suddenly a new and very large constituency to whom we were responsible. It was a global one, not just a national one, and it included the devout, atheists, agnostics, and those who were simply curious. It was therefore essential, in my view, that we do the most careful job of which we were capable, verifying everything again and again, going through the peer-review process, and publishing. The press would have to wait until we were done.

I returned to the testing. In Colorado Springs, Vern Miller had brought a large number of beautiful scientific photographs taken in Turin. Those taken by ultraviolet were most illuminating. At the margin of each scourge mark there was a pale white fluorescence that could not be seen in white light. It is typical of a lesion made by a whip that there will be an ooze of serum at the edges of the wound. Anyone who has skinned a knee will be familiar with this fact. There was a similar white fluorescence around the margin of the heavy blood flows. This, too, is physiologic. As part of the blood-clotting mechanism, the clot retracts after a while, squeezing out serum. The fibrils from these white fluorescent areas showed a positive test for protein by fluorescamine and by enzymatic test. We followed this up by using still another determination, Bromcreosol green, which gave us a positive test for albumin, the main proteinaceous component of blood. Thus, we could conclude that what was on the Shroud was whole blood. Microscopic amounts of blood were present as flakes, dots, blobs, and one other form that was interesting. Where the blood had coated fibrils and hardened, it had in many cases cracked off. These elongated, half-tubular replica casts of fibrils we called shards, since they looked like half-round roof tiles. We took specimens of the various types of blood shapes and did still another series of tests for blood, using potassium cyanide in ammonium hydroxide. This produced a positive result, giving the typical color of cyanomethemoglobin. We had noted that some of the shards had a greenish-brown color, which suggested to us that they might contain bile pigments; these are among the decay products of hemoglobin. We ran a specific assay, which gave us a characteristic blue-azobilirubin color. When acid was added, this became a paler purple and was discharged with UV light, giving still one more positive test for blood.

Thus far, our positive blood tests had included (1) microspectrophotometric scans of crystals and fibrils, (2) reflectance scans on the Shroud, (3) positive hemochromogen tests, (4) positive cyanomethemoglobin tests, (5) positive tests for bile pigments, and (6) characteristic heme porphyrin fluorescence. Any one of these is proof of the presence of blood, and each is acceptable in a court of law. Taken together, they are irrefutable.

This strong affirmation comes, in part, from my background. In 1954, I had founded a scientific society that now has chapters worldwide. The members are all concerned with a study of a very complex system in the body that performs a variety of exceedingly intricate functions. This system is called the reticuloendothelium. One of its functions is to make blood cells. For some years I had been occupied in making physical and chemical measurements of the functions of this system.

Adler has worked with heme porphyrins as well as other porphyrins, both in detection and synthesis.

When, with 100 percent certainty, we make a categorical statement that blood is present, believe it!

I have tested for the presence of blood in capital cases for the prosecution and defense. If I had found blood on two samples and one turned out to be Swiss cheese and the other a moon rock, I should, with confidence, tell the authorities to look for a gory dairyman or a wounded astronaut.

In science, we always try to challenge our own data. If there are any chinks in them that we do not find, someone else will — and that smarts.

"Suppose," I postulated to Adler, "some forger contrived a method to obtain fresh cow, pig, or sheep blood and painted like lightning to get the blood on the Shroud before it clotted. Let us further postulate that he knew enough about twentieth-century pathophysiology, fibrinogen, fibrin, platelets, and the like so that he painted all the wounds and bleeding correctly and . . ."

"Are you out of your mind?" asked Adler.

"The point I'm making," I went on, "is that we know that it's whole blood, but we don't know that it's *human* whole blood."

By this time we had used up most of the blood and serum fibrils. A test for human blood is relatively easy when you have an adequate amount, but making do with tiny samples is a hallmark of microchemistry.

To determine the species of animal from which a sample of protein is derived, we have to fall back on immunology. The basis of the test depends on the formation of antibodies. Antibodies are proteins that an individual's immune mechanism forms to neutralize any foreign material. This can include bacteria, viruses, or protein from another species. If we inject a small amount of human-serum albumin into a laboratory animal, it will make antihuman-albumin antibodies. Antibodies work in a manner akin to a key fitted to a complex lock. Every protein, including human-serum albumin, has a unique three-dimensional shape and is soluble in blood. Antibodies to the protein fit onto its shape with exquisite precision, like plaster of Paris poured over a statue. The resultant sculpture-cum-plaster is a totally different shape, and it is alien to the host body and insoluble. If we take the laboratory animal into which we have injected human-serum albumin, draw some blood, get rid of the blood cells, and add its serum to human serum, we will have a reaction. The human-albumin molecules will combine with the antibody and precipitate.

We decided to use one of the remaining serum-coated fibrils for the test. Some antihuman-albumin antibody was procured and a fluorescent tag attached to it. Bovine, porcine, and equine albumin were used as controls, and, as expected, were nonreactive. When the antibody to human protein was added to the fibril, it was strongly positive.

"O.K.," I said, "now we know it's human."

"Not necessarily," said Adler. "Some primate blood can cross-react and . . ."

"Stop it," I interrupted. "The painter would have had to cross to Africa, capture a chimp or a gorilla, return to Europe with it, and . . ."

"How about the Gibralter apes?"

I looked around for something to throw at him.

Now that the blood question had been tested as thoroughly and redundantly as we could do it, we decided to go forward to other determinations.

"What," asked Adler one day, "shall we test for in the way of elements?"

I decided to goad him. "All one hundred and eight of them," I shot back.

He merely growled.

Only about ninety elements occur naturally on earth. A couple more have been identified in certain stars. Others are synthetic, having been made in recent years in the nuclear laboratory; they are essentially unstable, and most vanish almost immediately. Testing for all of them would have been farcical.

We could, we figured, rule out a substantial use of any element in paint with an atomic weight over sixteen, because X-ray fluorescence would have caught it if it had been present in a significant amount. We needed to look for elements that, had they been present in small amounts, might have been missed by X-ray fluorescence or X radiography, and yet were present in sufficient amounts to be seen as color by the human eye. We finally agreed that testing for the following elements would be more than adequate: aluminum, arsenic, antimony, cadmium, calcium, cobalt, chromium, iron, nickel, mercury, manganese, lead, palladium, tin, zinc, and silver.

If dissecting a linen fibril had been a royal pain, excising particles was an imperial one. Almost all were very tiny. Once the scalpel hit the Mylar, the spatial distortion caused by the contact put the particle out of focus. From that point on, dimensional memory was the only thing I had to go on. After Adler washed off the adhesive, he would begin to remove the surplus solvent by dunking into the side of the dimple well very small, pointed pieces of filter paper, which would act like a blotter, sucking up the excess fluid. Extreme care had to be taken, because if the capillarity was too strong, the particle would disappear into the interstices of the filter paper, never to be seen again. During these tedious procedures, we always had to be sure that the particle was not a contaminant, like a piece of fly ash or a piece of insect wing. Once we had enough particles of a certain class — color, size, shape, optical characteristics — we would bring in our reagents for testing. These were primarily chemical complexes with such unmemorable names as 3-(4-phenyl-2 pyridyl)-5 phenyl-1,2,4-triazine disulfonic acid or p-dimethylaminobenzalrhodamine. Though our interest was centered on the nature of the red particles, we felt it was necessary to test all particles. In addition, it was possible that some elements were present in the form of a dye, in which a metal such as aluminum had been used as a mordant.

We decided to test all particles as well as fibrils in our search for elements that might provide a clue to color.

To be painstakingly thorough, we even decided to check the red blood particles for their iron content. Blood has iron in it, but only a thousandth of the mass of a hemoglobin molecule is iron; the rest of the molecule protects the iron from responding to a simple iron test. The red color is caused by the porphyrin structure. To free the iron, we would add a mixture that still goes by the old alchemists' name, aqua regia. It is made from concentrated nitric acid plus concentrated hydrochloric acid — powerful stuff indeed. Once aqua regia destroyed the porphyrin structure and the blood protein, we obtained a positive iron test — as we expected.

We decided to do the iron test on the fibrils to see how much iron had been deposited by the retting process. We took an off-image fibril, and it gave us a very strong positive for iron. Then we took an image fibril. It too was strongly positive for iron, as was scorched fiber. An iron test inside a water-stain area gave a weaker result than the others. The data were consistent with our retting-and-fire hypothesis. That triggered a thought. Since we found that the iron oxide was primarily in the water-stain margins, those margins should be more opaque to X rays. I called the radiographers on the team and asked them to check. They looked again at their X rays. Sure enough, those margins were more radiodense, as they had originally observed.

We also tested for calcium, and it checked out, strong and clear. We did not bother to check out the strontium, because that element is so similar chemically to calcium that once it is known to be present with calcium, it will stay there unless one decides to do something fancy to separate it.

However, it must be recalled that to check out an element

like calcium, we had to begin the test on one fiber, which took about an hour. All tests were done on a minimum of fifteen fibers, with controls each time, and on as many slides as provided the appropriate material; that is, image, blood, water stain, and so on. It was a time-consuming and arduous task.

Now that we were in full swing with elemental analysis, we could return to red particles. We knew that a microdrop of hydrazine would let us know rapidly if a particle was blood. If it was not, we would collect it for assay. If the particles were small — say, one micrometer (about 1/400,000th of an inch) — we might need as many as fifty of them for a metal test. It obviously took a long time to harvest that many. However, since I had decided that we would not rely on our eyesight to determine the identity of any microscopic object, we had to determine by physics and/or chemistry what the true nature of the object was. That put us in a Catch-22 situation. Harvesting enough particles for a test that would determine their nature required a bunch of particles. How could we tell which particles were alike before we made the test to see what they were?

First, we determined which of the red spots were blood. We proved that most of them were, because (1) they dissolved in hydrazine, (2) produced hemochromagen, a pale pink material, and (3) gave a positive test for protein. Iron oxide does none of these things. Nor does any other metal oxide or salt.

As I was harvesting red dots, I suddenly saw one that was not on the slide itself, but in the stickum alongside, where the adhesive had been squeezed out. This was an unusual particle compared with what I had been looking at, and was obviously a crystal.

I turned to Adler and said, "Look at this."

We traded places.

He said, "Do you know what this looks like?"

"Yup. Cinnabar."

I must not give the impression that I can look through a

microscope and reach geochemical conclusions by eye. I cannot. It just so happened that some years ago I was an expert witness in a case involving two countries and some purportedly stolen treasures. The key datum in the resolution was cinnabar, a mineral containing mercury sulfide.

Adler said, "Right. Let's test it."

While he was going after reagents in another laboratory, I studied the slide further. The piece of cinnabar was enormous compared with what we had been working with. I could actually pick it up with a microforceps. It was in the stickum at the side of the tape. Where had it come from? It was shaped like a pyramid with a broad base. After having measured the base, I began to manipulate the optics, the light sources, and I finally convinced myself that I could see a track across a corner of the slide where the crystal had been dragged. There were extremely tiny fragments that had abraded off the base. When Adler returned with the proper chemicals, we obtained a strong, positive test for mercury. This, together with its crystalline structure, proclaimed it to be cinnabar. Out of this material the color vermilion is made. It has been much favored by artists through the ages; Rubens, for example, used it extensively.

We had heard through the grapevine that Walter McCrone was publishing a third paper in *The Microscope*, in which he claimed that the presence of vermilion proved conclusively that the Shroud was a painted forgery.

Well, we had just found a piece — a crystal — of cinnabar, and that certainly confirmed that there was at least one particle of vermilion on the Shroud.

13

Necessary and Sufficient Proof

WE HAD NOW FOUND iron oxide and mercury sulfide. Both are pigments used by artists. Both are red.

To determine whether an artifact is painted, the first thing that a scientific detective will do is find out whether any paint pigment is present. If it is, and if the presence of such pigment is the only standard, a man may well feel that the problem is solved. The artifact is a painting.

However, science demands particular criteria for proof of anything. One criterion is embodied in the words "necessary and sufficient." In order to establish that something is a painted object, it is "necessary" to show colorants. However, that is not "sufficient." It must be shown that there is sufficient paint to account for the object one sees in the painting, such as a house or a tree. We had just discovered one crystal of mercury (and its track), and like the hounds after the hare, we began a complete and exhaustive search for additional samples. On that tape, and on all the rest, there was not another one.

It was McCrone's claim that the images were made of red ocher — also an artist's pigment — and gelatin. We could find neither. It was also his contention that the blood was not blood, but red iron oxide. We found blood — lots of it — by many different methods in the blood areas. And the only area in which there was iron oxide was in the water-stain margins.

It was now 1981, three years after the team's trip to Turin. McCrone sent me a Xerograph of his third paper. In it, he stated that the blood was paint, a mixture of iron oxide and mercury sulfide. He claimed that he had found nine microscopic particles of vermilion. Necessary? Yes. Sufficient? No. There was not enough iron oxide or vermilion to account for one painted drop of blood, let alone all the gore on the Shroud.

After Adler read McCrone's third *Microscope* paper, he was speechless — a rare and unusual state for him. When he finally sputtered his way back to coherence, he asked, "Say, isn't red ocher almost always impure?"

I mulled it over.

"Yes. It seems to me that I remember it's always contaminated with manganese, nickel, cobalt, or aluminum."

"That's how I remember it. Let's test the iron oxide for impurities. If all the iron on the Shroud comes either from the retting process or from blood, it should be pure; if it comes from ground deposits, as red ocher does, it should have at least one of those contaminants in it."

It was really gilding the lily yet again to carry out these determinations, but considering the nature of this project, we decided not only to gild but to platinum-plate it. First, of course, we had to find out the usual level of the red ocher contaminants. This was not easy, since they vary from deposit to deposit. I consulted geochemists, who all agreed that iron oxide was indeed contaminated, but when I asked the percentage of contamination, they usually answered that they did not know and wondered why anyone would want to know such an outlandish fact.

Finally, after consulting old texts in English, German, French, Italian, and Swedish, we had reasonable mini-max values for the level of these contaminants. They should be present above the 1 percent level. That was good enough for a start. By wet chemistry we could determine the levels.

We began to gather microscopic red iron-oxide dots. After what seemed forever, we had enough. We set up a solution of silver with catalyzed acid persulfate, dimethyl glyoxime, nioxime, ammonium thiocyanate and fluoride, plus Aluminon and alizarin. There were no contaminants at the 1 percent level. Adler was delighted. I was not. I wanted to be sure that the other elements were not present at all. I decided to do an electron microprobe test.

First, I isolated iron-oxide particles from several tapes and put them on aluminum stubs. The stubs were placed in the scanning electron microscope, and the image appeared on a CRT. The image is similar to what one sees on a black and white TV screen. Magnifications of up to 100,000 times or more can be made. Once the iron-oxide particle was in place, an attachment that permits elemental analysis by electron microprobe was activated. This operates in a manner not unlike an X-ray machine: a tiny beam of electrons hits the particle, X rays are emitted at different energies, and, in effect, one sees a spectrum of different peaks — the unique fingerprints of various elements. These peaks appear on another CRT and are displayed in colored graphics. There is a baseline that indicates what wavelengths of X rays are being produced at different energies in kilovolts. Certain peaks at certain kilovoltages are indicative of particular elements. Markers, which indicate where certain peaks should appear if the element you are seeking is present, can be called to the screen via computer. In this case, I set up cobalt, manganese, nickel, and aluminum. I kicked in the Kevex ISI 100B Energy Dispersive Spectrometer and watched the screen. Since the beam was hitting an iron-oxide particle, a strong iron signal immediately appeared, but I ignored it, since I knew iron was present. It was the other peaks that I was looking for. The process continued for 120 seconds. This is a long time for this process, more than enough to indicate whether something is present or absent. The iron peak had long since gone way off scale, and there were no "contaminants" present. I repeated this procedure with each of the particles placed on the stubs. The iron was pure, and hence not a derivative from some hematite deposit in the Old World.

It was now that Professor Riggi's decision to join the team proved important again and complemented our present research. Back in Turin, he had obtained some samples of Venetian red from Renaissance sources. Riggi put these samples in an electron microprobe, and, sure enough, there were strong peaks of our four contaminants. Then Riggi obtained fresh, modern Venetian red, and the same contaminants appeared. Thus, iron earth pigments, whether new or old, contained the same contaminants. The iron oxide on the Shroud did not contain any of them. Riggi's control experiment bore out the results of ours.

John Jackson had come up with an interesting hypothesis early in the research. As mentioned earlier, he suggested that the Shroud had been folded so many times that particles may have been transposed from their original site. That is exactly what we found. The blood had abraded off in many places and was transposed everywhere. It was blood that accounted for most of the red dots on the body image fibrils. To check Jackson's theory, I took out the Spanish linen with my blood on it; the fabric had been folded and unfolded. Sure enough, under the microscope, tiny blood particles could be seen all over.

McCrone had also mentioned that he had seen "orpiment, ultramarine, azurite, wood charcoal, and madder rose." He did not cite any experimental evidence other than that *he saw them.* We examined every particle type we could find and tested it chemically, and could not corroborate any of his observations.

We continued to look for other metallic species, but the only ones we found were represented by extremely minute black dots. They were located primarily around burn holes in the scorch area and gave a strong positive test for silver. They were obviously spatter from the molten silver drops that had burned through the cloth in 1532. They were far too scanty to have been picked up by X-ray fluorescence, as, of course, was the case for the mercury sulfide. Nor could such minute amounts produce any color that could be seen by eye. Naturally, there was carbon from the fire.

Adler and I had now arrived at a point where we had exhausted all the possibilities of any other reasonable (and some unreasonable) metallic species being present. This may sound straightforward; in actual fact, it had taken us months.

It was time to get down to what I considered the serious testing for straw-yellow fibrils so that we could determine the nature of the color. As a first step, we decided we had better find out whether there were any fats or oils responsible for the color of the image fibrils. That was easy. We checked with the Hanus' and Wij's iodine-addition reagents. There was none.

Now we had arrived at the part we were reasonably sure would answer the question "What chemical made the straw-yellow images?" We had disagreed with McCrone that the images were made of gelatin and iron oxide, but could not yet disagree that the images were man-made. Unless and until we found out why the images were colored, we would not know that answer.

Testing for the straw-yellow color, however, would be much more complicated than testing for blood. But once we could identify the yellow paint or pigment, or dye or stain, we might know a lot more about how the images had been made and how they came to be on the cloth.

All organic colors, whether natural or synthetic, fall into three categories. In the first group are those which will change color in an acid or a base (alkali). In the second are those which will change either with oxidation or reduction (the opposite of oxidation). Finally, there are those which can be extracted with one of a large series of organic solvents, such as methanol, ethanol, benzene, toluene, acetone, carbon tetrachloride, pyridine, ethyl acetate, dimethyl formamide.

First, we tried to extract the color with concentrated hydrochloric acid. No change. Then we tried concentrated sulfuric acid. No change.

We were still doing all tests against controls. When we used the sulfuric-acid extraction on the tan Coptic linen (A.D. 350) and the brown Pharaonic linen (1500 B.C.), the color came right off. I had no idea what the color was and did not really care.

Then we went to alkaline solutions. We used concentrated ammonium hydroxide and strong potassium hydroxide, with no effect at all. Next in line was a powerful oxidant, 30 percent hydrogen peroxide. What one buys in a pharmacy is either 3 percent or 6 percent; the 30 percent variety is very dangerous material and must be handled with great care. Only one drop on your flesh is nasty. The peroxide caused no change. After that, we tried an ordinary reducing material, ascorbate, still with no result.

We made some specific tests for certain classes of organic compounds — phenols, flavenoids, steroids, indoles, lignins, porphyrins, pyrroles, nitroderivatives, and *Saponaria* extract (soapwort), to mention but a few.

We had increased our knowledge of what the yellow color was not. Now we had to see whether we could extract it with different types of solvents. One by one, extraction systems were set up and tried — dioxane, morpholine, ether, cyclohexane, dimethyl formamide, ethyl acetate, pyridine, chloroform, carbon tetrachloride, acetone . . . Absolutely none extracted or changed the color.

At the end of months of work, we had pretty well eliminated all paints, pigments, dyes, and stains. Where did this leave us? There were images of a man that produced 3-D read-outs in a VP-8, and the images were not the result of any colorant that had been added. Obviously, our next step was to examine whether there had been any intrinsic change in the cellulose structure of the linen itself.

The first thing to look for in anything that is old is oxidation. Oxidation refers to the process whereby something reacts with oxygen. Oxygen is a very potent reactant, and almost anything that is exposed to it will oxidize and deteriorate, as iron becomes rust. About 20 percent of the earth's atmosphere is oxygen. If it were not for a peculiar circumstance of this planet, oxygen would react rapidly with all manner of things and leave the atmosphere made up of nothing but nitrogen and a few other gases. That circumstance is green plant life, which continuously produces oxygen from an oxide of carbon.

Cellulose, as we have seen, is a biopolymer of sugar. It can oxidize in an almost bewildering number of ways, depending on conditions. Since Adler and I knew very little about all the conditions to which the cloth might have been subjected since its fabrication, we could not assume anything.

If the straw-yellow of the images was the result of oxidation, we thought, we should be able to reverse the process with reductants. We had used ascorbate but had seen no change. Perhaps it was not a strong enough reducing agent, so we decided to use diimide, which is a potent one. If that did not show any change, we could forget about oxidation. A droplet of diimide was added to a straw-yellow fibril and instantly became white. At last, after two years of puzzling about the yellow, we had a positive test! Necessary? Yes. Sufficient? No. We began to look at oxidative intermediate reactions. This necessitated thrashing through such items as acetal, hemiacetal, aldol condensation (intra- and inter-), ester formation, and on and on. Finally, after working with many types of intermediates, we wound up with an aldol condensation that, on dehydration, gave an alpha, beta unsaturated carbonyl, which in turn went to a conjugated carbonyl (or alpha dicarbonyl groups). This probably sounds as exciting as a wet dishrag, but to us it was exhilarating. This conjugated carbonyl has a color. It is straw-yellow!

The conjugated carbonyl is the end product of dehydrating acid oxidation. (By contrast, alkaline oxidation produces no color.) We felt that we should be able, therefore, to make a pseudo-image fibril by immersing it long enough in concentrated sulfuric acid, which is a strong dehydrative oxidant fluid, in addition to being a powerful acid. We began by using nonimage background fibrils. After thirty minutes in sulfuric acid, they had the right color and chemistry of an image fibril. Using a special type of microscopic observation (phase contrast), we could readily observe that the image fibrils were much more corroded than the nonimage fibrils. The sulfuric acid–treated fibrils looked identical with the image fibrils under phase contrast microscopy. We also made pseudo-image fibrils from the Spanish linen and other control linens.

In sum, the microscopic corrosion of the pseudo-image fibrils was correct, as were the straw-yellow color and the chemistry and the physical infrared observations. We had a match.

Now all we had to figure out was how a selective dehydrative acid oxidizing agent got on the Shroud in such a manner as to produce images of a man that in a VP-8 were 3-D!

I have always wanted to do an experiment whose result was so overwhelmingly positive and definitive that I could shout "Eureka." It does not seem to work that way. Months and months of painstaking experiment with endless repeats is the slow and progressive norm. It feels just as good, but it is not explosive.

At this point, I decided to carry out some *gedankenexperiments*. A favorite ploy of Albert Einstein's, gedankenexperiment literally means "thought experiment." One attacks a problem by setting up a series of events and constraints, and then solves the problem in one's head, rather than in the laboratory. By a series of flukes, Einstein had been my unofficial undergraduate adviser. Once or twice every year, I would travel from Yale to Princeton to seek counsel. On one of those occasions Einstein told me that I should always remember that a gedankenexperiment requires a very small research budget.

For numerous reasons, Adler and I had been assuming all along that the Shroud was a forgery. Any hypothesis based on contact between the Shroud and body chemicals had to be ruled out, because the physics of the images seemed to preclude it. Forgery (painting, block print, or such) was something that *could* be tested for. If the images on the Shroud were man-made, we could rule in or out the various possibilities. I make that statement with an extraordinarily high confidence level. We both believed it at the beginning of our research, and we believe it now.

We sat down and began to brainstorm. What would have been the constraints on an artist who decided to paint the Shroud? During the 120 hours that the team examined the Shroud, they observed that the straw-yellow of the images was confined to the surface fibrils only. In no circumstances did the color penetrate more than two or three fibrils. And it was confined to their crests. The hue of each straw-yellow fibril was essentially the same as all the rest. It was merely the *numbers* of fibrils that gave the impression of darker or lighter areas. This was a very important point, for the VP-8 is a modified computer. It can assess things quantitatively. The images of the man on the Shroud were encoded in the number of fibrils, which is why the VP-8 could "read" them.

This is radically different from the way any imaging works in our everyday world. For example, our eyes see objects, including people, by an albedo image — by the light that is reflected. A photograph also picks up an albedo image from the light reflected off the surface. An artist sees an albedo image and portrays it on his canvas. If he is painting a landscape with foreground and background, he uses perspective. A VP-8 cannot handle the world of albedo images and perspective, but it can and does handle quanta of light. In effect, it sees numerically, not reflectively. The images on the Shroud are numerical, as well as reversed, as in a photographic negative.

With all this in mind, Adler and I began a gedankenexperiment to see what would be required of an artist. As mentioned earlier, you cannot see the man in the Shroud unless you are one or two meters away. An artist cannot paint if he cannot see what effect his brush is producing. Our putative artist, then, must have had a paintbrush one to two meters long. It must have consisted of a single bristle, since it painted single fibrils that were 10 to 15 microns in diameter. The finest paintbrush bristles I know of are sable, and a sable hair is vast in diameter compared with a linen fibril. In addition, the artist would have had to figure out a paint medium that had no oil or water, because there were no indications of capillarity. Now, to see what he was painting he would have needed a microscope with an enormous focal length that would permit the brush to operate under it. The physics of optics preclude such a device, unless it is attached to a television set. In this case, it would have had to be a color TV, for the straw-yellow is too faint to register on black and white.

Another constraint the artist must have dealt with is the limit of the human nervous system. No one can hold so long a brush steady enough to paint the top of a fibril. One would need a twentieth-century micromanipulator, which would have to work hydraulically at a distance of one to two meters. It would have to be rigged to a device called a waldo, which is an invention of the atomic era. Also, the artist would have to know how many fibrils to paint quantitatively, and do the whole thing in reverse, like a negative.

Our hypothetical artist obviously must have used blood — both pre-mortem and post-mortem. And he had to paint with serum albumin alongside the edges of the scourge marks. Since serum albumin is visible only under ultraviolet, not white light, he had to paint with an invisible medium. If an artist had painted the Shroud, the blood must have been put on after the images. We decided to check that point. We took some blood- and serum-covered fibrils from a body image area. If the images were there before the blood, and if we removed the blood, we could expect to see straw-yellow image fibers. We prepared a mixture of enzymes that digest blood and its proteins. When all the blood and protein were gone, the underlying fibrils were not straw-yellow; they were ordinary background fibrils. This was strong evidence that the blood had gone on before the images. It suggested that blood had protected the linen from the image-making process. Surely this was a weird way to paint a picture.

Obviously, no one can paint with sulfuric acid, because it would destroy the bristle, would show signs of capillarity, and have all the other constraints of our gedankenexperiment. Heat can cause the same kind of oxidation as sulfuric acid, but any heat source radiates in a diffuse manner, and cannot account for the resolution or the three-dimensionality seen in the features of the face of the man in the Shroud or the microprecision of the color on the crests of only the straw-yellow fibrils.

How about other image-making techniques, such as two giant block prints, each one two meters long and one meter wide, and heated? Stone was used for block prints in the medieval period. If you put sulfuric acid on a stone, the acid reacts immediately and destroys the stone; the same, of course, applies to wood or metal. Aside from a vast series of technical improbabilities in accomplishing such madness, we could think of no other possibility. There were a few other really strange ideas, such as hot statues, bas-reliefs, and so on, suggested by nonscientists, but these had long since been examined and rejected, because they could be ruled out — both theoretically and experimentally.

Finally, I told Adler that, ignoring whatever artistic method might have been used, the artist would have had to crucify somebody to get the pathophysiology just right. Emperor Constantine had outlawed crucifixion in the fourth century. Western and Byzantine art depictions of crucifixions are medically incorrect. Our presumptive artist, however, knew what was correct, and outside of crucifying a few people to get the anatomy and pathophysiology right, he could hardly have come by this arcane knowledge.

I recognize that human capability can incise a page of text on the head of a pin, that Michelangelo painted the Sistine Chapel, probably on his back by candlelight, and that man can accomplish extraordinary works of genius. But these works have to be within the limits set by the laws of physics and chemistry. How could a man create reversed, monochrome images with numerical data encoded with acid or heat?

Along with the rest of the team, we tackled this question. It is in our nature and our training to refuse to accept the mystical as an explanation of an object. The Shroud is an object — palpable, measurable. Well, we had measured, and done so *in extenso*. We would just have to persevere until we had the answer to the question "How did the images get there?"

With this question still very much in mind, Adler and I had arrived at the point where we could begin to write a paper that would cover all the chemical studies done on the Shroud. Normally, writing a scientific paper is quite easy. One writes a short introduction, followed by a section on methods and materials. This is followed by results, a brief discussion, and a conclusion. Under conventional circumstances, this poses no problem: an experiment is designed to tackle a specific problem; the methodology is normally clear-cut; the results can often be portrayed in one or two graphs or tables. Our paper on the presence of blood on the Shroud had been written in three days in just this form and was published in *Applied Optics*. The paper we were now contemplating, however, had over a thousand experiments to report and a plethora of findings, both positive and negative. It covered a host of tests, and it had to address and refute the findings of McCrone. Because of the controversial nature of the subject, the paper had to be airtight, capable of withstanding the critical survey not only of other members of STURP and the review board of the journal, but also of other scientists from all over the world. It was a daunting prospect.

And what would be the appropriate journal? Our subject matter covered so many disciplines that there was no single publication within whose purview such a complex article would fit. It was archeological chemistry, as well as organic and inorganic chemistry. It pertained to analytical chemistry. There were significant studies having to do with wounds and blood, so it could have been submitted to a journal on pathology. There was biochemistry, botany, and textile chemistry, too.

While we were debating the problem, I received a telephone call from the chairman of the upcoming annual meeting of the Canadian Society of Forensic Sciences. He told me that the society had decided to hold a plenary session on the Shroud of Turin at the meeting. He had invited McCrone, who had accepted. Also invited were Dr. Robert Bucklin and Dr. John Jackson. Would Adler and I be willing to present our work? The society further asked that we publish our paper in its journal. This was a fortuitous solution to our problem.

I was delighted. Here was a chance to have a discussion with McCrone, face to face, on his substantive findings and on ours. The meeting of the Canadian Society of Forensic Sciences would be an ideal forum.

Everyone was pleased that we would finally have the opportunity to meet with McCrone and try to sort out our very substantial differences. While we were preparing slides and tables for our presentation, we received word from the society that there would be a host of reporters there from key scientific journals. It was shaping up to be a climactic event.

14

Science and the Image

In May of 1981, three months before the August conclave of the Canadian Society of Forensic Sciences, Tom D'Muhala, who had succeeded Jackson as president of STURP, called a meeting.

One of the agenda items was the form of a wrap-up paper. Jumper favored a "results" paper, in which all the findings would be taken and correlated and conclusions drawn. Jackson preferred a logic-tree format. Such a paper would state that (1) the Shroud was made by eye/brain/hand, or (2) it was not. If it was not, then it must have been made by (a) body contact, or (b) some other method. The logic tree would keep ramifying.

It was decided to do both types. Schwalbe would do the logic tree, and Jumper would do the results paper.

Then Adler and I presented our chemical work. We had brought 450 microphotographs, and it became a show-and-tell session. Everyone demanded rigorous justification: chemical, physical, spectral, kinetic, thermodynamic, biologic, mathematical, and statistical. It took six hours. The implications of our work, combined with everyone else's results, were unattractive, because they left no reasonable explanation as to how the images came to be on the cloth. We had gone into this research with a firm conviction that, given the time, tools, and facilities, science would unquestionably answer the two key questions:

1. What were the bloodstains and body images made of?
2. How were they formed?

We believed that once we knew the answer to the first question, we would, ipso facto, have the answer to the second. There was no doubt about it. Except that it was not working out that way. The blood was blood, and the images were the result of a conjugated carbonyl of the cellulose. It was imperative that we now address the problem of "how" with all possible scientific rigor.

Adler and I had reached the conclusion that the images could not have been made by artistic endeavor. Jackson, Jumper, and Ercoline had tackled the problem by asking the same question in a slightly different way. Could the images have been made by eye/brain/hand? Their approach was physical, as opposed to chemical.

They began by analyzing the 3-D images in the VP-8. It is only when *actual* depth or remoteness is manifest by less light that the VP-8 can produce an authentic 3-D picture.

Could an artist produce a 3-D image? There are paintings that were made from the Shroud itself by some of the masters. In the VP-8, they are dimensional disasters. To take experimentation and measurement one step further, Jackson, Jumper, and Ercoline obtained the services of some police artists, who copied the Shroud as faithfully as they could. The results in the VP-8 were badly contorted. Then they had the artists draw from the 3-D VP-8 images. Again, the VP-8 images were seriously aberrant.

At this point, the investigators took a different tack. They procured a life-size plaster bust of a bearded man. A photograph of the statue put in the VP-8 produced a badly misshapen image. They coated the bust with phosphorescent paint, and the outcome was worse. Ingeniously, they contrived an experiment to encode brightness and dimness as authentic distance dimensions. They took the bust, still with the phosphorescent coating, and submerged it, nose up, in a large container of dilute black ink. The nose, which was closest to the top of the inky solution, was brighter; the eye sockets and the hairline, darker. A photograph of the surface of that liquid, when placed in the VP-8, produced an *authentic* 3-D image of the head.

They then went on to test the hypotheses based on the hot statue, block print, engraving, and bas-relief transfer. All resulted in seriously deformed images.

They carried their analysis further. They went to a stereometric laboratory, where they placed a volunteer of the same stature and weight as the man in the Shroud on a glass-topped table. They crawled beneath to make measurements and photographs and saw that the weight of the man caused a flattening of certain areas. Over the shoulder blades there were two bilaterally symmetrical, almost trapezoidal flat areas, just as seen in the VP-8 image of the back.

There was also flattening of both buttocks, thighs, and calves. One leg made an impression identical with that seen in the VP-8. The other did not. Jumper looked at the front image of the VP-8 and saw that one knee was slightly raised. They raised the knee of the volunteer so that the sheet covering him showed the same amount of prominence. There was a proportionate marginal rounding of the thigh and calf of the partly flexed leg, and now the subject's back and the VP-8 back image were alike. To my knowledge, these nuances could not have been known by anyone who did not do the glass-table experiment.

Nor was this the end of it. On the hands there appear only four digits. The thumbs are missing. It may not be "artistic," but it is neurological. If a spike is driven through the wrist between the radius and ulna, it is likely that the ulnar nerve will be damaged, which will cause the thumb to flex acutely into the palm of the hand. Rigor mortis would keep it that way. The fingers in the Shroud image are longer than average, but they are still within the normal range (Gaussian distribution). This may be reasonable anatomy, but it is not, I suggest, reasonable for an artist. One wrist is not seen on the Shroud. When the volunteer crossed his hands and flexed the thumb of the upper hand, the cloth tented at about a two-inch distance from the lower wrist. All the above, including the blood and wound pathophysiology, require knowledge not known until the nineteenth century and demand artistic information available only from *inside* the Shroud covering both sides of a corpse. The conclusion of the physical scientists was that the Shroud could not be the result of eye/brain/hand.

They had come to the conclusion that Adler and I had reached through a different route.

We went on to examine the possibility that some chemicals from the body formed the images on the Shroud. The chemicals could be substances produced by the body or added to the body, such as an anointing fluid. The interaction of both also must be considered. This was not too promising an avenue, for had there been substances on the body, which was lying on its back, the rear image would have been more saturated than the front one. It was not.

Adler and I had found no traces of aloe, myrrh, or any other spice. We had found no oils, though they may have oxidized away.

Sam Pellicori, a champion of the body-contact hypothesis, had done some interesting experiments. In three separate experiments, he had placed oil, lemon juice, and perspiration on his fingers. Then he placed linen on top of his hand and pressed it gently to his flesh. He then placed the cloth samples in an oven at low temperature to produce an accelerated aging effect. In each case there was indeed a yellowing of the contact area. He had brought the linen samples with him. The team examined them and, although there was a surface effect, several of us insisted that we could see some capillarity in several of the fibrils, which is not the case on the Shroud. We all agreed with Sam that the torso of the man had had to be in contact with the Shroud, or the transfer of the scourge marks would not have appeared as they did. For example, there were many such lesions that were invisible in white light and could be seen only in the UV. The hemoglobin and serum ooze could have come only from direct contact. However, the recessed areas of the face could not have been in contact with the cloth, as proved by the VP-8 images and the Shroud-body distance data. Pellicori agreed that that was still a problem for his hypothesis. It was not *a* problem, but rather *the* problem. However, as a group we raised every reasonable and even unreasonable chemical hypothesis and scenario. One by one, each was destroyed. There seemed no apparent or even remote chemical mechanism produced by a body with and without anointing oil that could explain the image formation.

It was evident from the physical, mathematical, medical, and chemical evidence that there must have been a crucified man in the Shroud. If we followed the principle of Occam's razor, we could draw no other conclusion. William of Occam had stated six centuries ago a principle of parsimony that is dear to the heart of scientists. It states that if there is a simple way of arriving at an explanation, contrasted to a complicated one, the simpler is probably correct.

How were the images of the man conveyed to the linen? Virtually the only mechanism left was radiation, which we then examined. The first candidate was ionizing radiation. Included under this heading are gamma rays, X rays, ultraviolet plus energetic particles, such as electrons and alphas. Ionizing radiation produces alkaline oxidation, not the acid form. I had exposed linen to six hours of intense ultraviolet radiation and found no acid oxidation and no straw-yellow color. Furthermore, most ionizing radiation is very hard or penetrating. As such, it will not be attenuated by air. If the man was, by some unknown mechanism, emitting radiation, the rays from the noncontact areas — the space under the nose and the eye sockets, for example — must have been partly absorbed by air before they hit the cloth. Otherwise, we would have no distance information in the VP-8. In addition, radiation from a source radiates in all directions (isotropic), as it does from a light bulb. The only time it is unidirectional and parallel is when it comes from a laser. The bust covered with phosphorescent paint looked like a light bulb in the VP-8. Only the black inky fluid attenuated the light. However, visible light causes no chemical change in linen, so we could not have the cadaver in inky water as a mechanism. Ultrasoft X rays and radiowaves are attenuated by water, but that got us nowhere. We had just about exhausted the electromagnetic spectrum.

We turned once more to heat. A hot bas-relief — of all the models measured by the physicists — gave some distance information, but it was seriously flawed. When the bas-relief was hot enough to cause the recessed areas to show on linen, the hot spots, like the tip of the nose, burned through the cloth. Considering the heat conductivity of linen — wet or dry — the mechanism did not work.

We had now reviewed all the new and the old experiments. The only possible mechanisms were molecular transport and radiation, and we had just demolished both of them. This was extremely unsettling. The weekend had come to an end, and we all headed homeward in a pensive mood.

A few days later, I received a call from Father Adam Otterbein. His mentor, and the man who had kindled his interest in the Shroud, was Father Wuenschel. After Father Wuenschel's death, the huge collection of research data on the Shroud he had amassed during his lifetime was catalogued and kept in the seminary at Esopus, New York. I had told Father Otterbein that I would like to look over this collection sometime. After all, you can never tell what you may find.

Father Otterbein fixed a time, and Adler, who loves old collections of anything printed, came with me. The enormous amount of material collected by Father Wuenschel ranged from photocopies or hand copies of volumes out of the Vatican library holdings to municipal records from France and Italy to incunabula: notes, essays, manuscripts.

If Father Wuenschel was in Germany when he collected something, his notes would be in German; in France, French; in Turin, Italian; in Rome, Latin. I came across a group of woodcut prints of dozens and dozens of clerics, each holding the Shroud. (Small wonder that there was such a mélange of fibrils on it.)

As we burrowed further, we found that at least sixty artists — Van Dyke and Rubens among them — had painted the Shroud from "life." We already knew the proclivity of viewers of the Shroud to touch something to the cloth. It was a safe bet that some of these artists had placed their finished work on the Shroud. An artist painting in the same room as the Shroud would be enough to explain such microscopic "accidentals" as a speck of vermilion from a palette or brush. I had experienced this in the early days of the atomic era. Back in the early fifties I was the radiation safety officer at Yale. I had been called in on an outside consultation. An overly enthusiastic artist had decided to do a painting on canvas with luminous paint. He had used a mixture of radium and thorium with a phosphor, a chemical that glows when activated by energetic radiation. The radium and thorium emit electrons, alpha particles, and gamma rays. (It was this formula which was used on old-fashioned luminous dial watches.) When I entered the room where the artist had been painting, I found that the spatter and spray from his brush were almost everywhere, and the radioactive contamination was ferocious.

If we added this spatter factor to the fact that many artists touched their finished product to the Shroud, the finding of such accidentals is not only logical, but virtually mandatory.

August was now approaching. By now, the Canadian Forensic Society had our paper. It included over a thousand individual experiments, would turn out to be twenty-two printed pages long, and was the most difficult writing chore either Adler or I had ever undertaken. It cleared the last of the peer reviewers, was accepted, and was scheduled for publication in September 1981. But first would come the August debate with McCrone at the plenary session of the society, in Hamilton, Ontario.

Doctors John Jackson, Robert Bucklin, Alan Adler, and I would present the physical, forensic, and chemical data. Dr. McCrone would present his forgery conclusions. Everyone's anticipation grew, for this was a proper scientific forum, and we knew that the scientific press also had made reservations to be there.

Unfortunately, the confrontation did not take place. McCrone decided not to attend, and sent an assistant in his stead. The assistant had not done the work, so he could only repeat what was in McCrone's papers, which everyone already knew. Nor did the scientific press appear. During the question period from the audience, someone asked McCrone's assistant, "Heller and Adler found blood, and you claim it's iron oxide. How do you explain that?"

"We're particle experts, not blood experts."

Then Adler and I presented our data on iron oxide. It was in the water-stain margins, and not elsewhere — definitely not in the images and blood areas, except where the water-stain margins intersected them.

Adler was asked, "Your data and McCrone's are at variance, aren't they?"

He replied, "Apparently."

And with that, the epic collision ended. It was neither epic nor a collision.

The final meeting of STURP was set for New London in the fall of 1981, and it would be historic, from the point of view of the scientists. It would mark the third anniversary of their five days of work on the Shroud in Turin. Though we had published our results in the scientific literature, it was at the end of three years that we had promised to report to the public on all of our work. This gathering would mark the last time that all of the STURP team would meet together as a unit. There was an *ave atque vale* air about the rendez-vous.

The site of the meeting was the main auditorium of Connecticut College. McCrone was invited to take part, but he declined once more. Among those present were visitors from England, France, Holland, Belgium, Germany, Italy, Switzerland, Brazil, Mexico, Japan, and Portugal. They had come to hear the report of the scientists and to view a perfectly magnificent photographic exhibition created by the Brooks Institute. Even though the assemblage of these unusual and powerful photographs had cost Brooks in the vicinity of $30,000, the key contributors, Ernie Brooks, Vern Miller, and Barrie Schwortz, had stipulated that there must never be any charge to those who wished to see it. Booking requests had already been received from all over the United States, the Philippines, Ireland, Italy, and Mexico. Descriptions of the cloth may be eloquent, but when one sees the life-size five-foot, eleven-inch images of the bloodied man — both positive and negative, front and back — it becomes clear that mere words are inadequate. Also shown was the image-enhancement work with pseudocolor, and various investigators at work on the project with their instrumentation. And in the background there was music recorded at the Cathedral of St. John in Turin, the home of the Shroud. The exhibit was impressive. When it was first shown in Santa Barbara, and subsequently in New London, tens of thousands of people, by actual count, poured in week after week. Neither place is exactly at the world's crossroads.

The scientists were asked to make their presentations in language comprehensible to the layman. I suspect that all of us were somewhat daunted by the task, because a lot of the material was so complex that English substitutions for some of the scientific nomenclature and processes simply did not exist. No one knew how the others were going to handle their portions, so, to an extent, we were all flying blind. Each of us would have ten to twenty minutes. After each presentation, there would be questions from the audience.

Finally, there would be a press conference. There were over three hundred representatives of the printed and electronic media.

We began our presentation. One by one, we gave our short talks with slides, graphs, spectra, and tried to make them intelligible to the nonscientist. Everything that had been done was included, from mathematical models, VP-8 and physical experiments, to pathology.

Early on, one of the questioners referred to himself and the audience as the "real people" and to us as the "Shroud crowd." We thought that was fair enough, and we did our best to communicate with the real people. We explained that we hoped to obtain permission to do a carbon 14 dating test some time in the future, but we had not yet received permission.

We all wanted to be very careful that we did not overstate anything. We were extremely cautious to make no statement of any kind that could not be supported by the data. Bit by bit, the complex story involving optics, mathematics, physics, chemistry, biology, and medicine unfolded. Most of the questions were excellent.

Adler was asked how he could answer McCrone's claim that there was no blood, but merely a mixture of red ocher and vermilion. Adler flashed on the screen the following table from our paper.

Table 5

Tests confirming the presence of whole blood on the Shroud

1. High iron in blood areas by X-ray fluorescence
2. Indicative reflection spectra
3. Indicative microspectrophotometric transmission spectra
4. Chemical generation of characteristic porphyrin fluorescence
5. Positive hemochromogen tests
6. Positive cyanomethemoglobin tests
7. Positive detection of bile pigments

8. Positive demonstration of protein
9. Positive indication of albumin
10. Protease tests, leaving no residue
11. Positive immunological test for human albumin
12. Microscopic appearance as compared with appropriate controls
13. Forensic judgment of the appearance of the various wound and blood marks

Then, after explaining each item briefly, Al said, "That means that the red stuff on the Shroud is emphatically, and without any reservation, nothing else but B-L-O-O-D!"

Many people in the audience and in the press asked, in more ways than I thought were possible, whether the scientific evidence indicated that the Shroud was the authentic burial cloth of Jesus.

We thought we had answered this question as many times as it was asked. Finally, Ray Rogers took the floor.

"In science, you're entitled to any hypothesis you choose, including the one that the Shroud was made by elves from the Black Forest. But if you don't have a test to examine that hypothesis, it's not worth anything. We do not have a test for Jesus Christ. So we can't hypothesize or test for that question."

It did not work. The question still came, over and over: "But do you *think* it is authentic?"

We would reply, "That's not a scientific question. We're here to present the scientific findings. We can't answer that question."

Our most difficult problem came from some members of the press. They seemed to want short, pithy answers, where they did not exist. One chap decided to by-pass Joan Janney, who was chairing the meeting, and demanded of the forty scientists seated on the stage, "All who believe this is the authentic Shroud of Christ, raise your hands."

Forty pairs of eyes just stared at him.

"O.K.," he said, "all those who don't believe it's authentic, raise your hands."

Forty of us sat still; none moved. He was frustrated and hostile.

At that point, one of the real people asked, "Have you found anything that would preclude the Shroud's being authentic?"

"No."

And that question is not a trivial one. Nothing in all the findings of the Shroud crowd in three years contained a single datum that contravened the Gospel accounts. The stigmata on the body did not follow art or legend. They were of life. They were medically accurate evidence of a man who had been scourged with a flagrum-type device, both front and back, by two men; who had carried something rough and heavy across his shoulders, which had been bruised; who had had something placed on his head that had caused punctate bleeding wounds over the scalp and forehead; who had lesions on nose and knee commensurate with a fall; who had been beaten about the face; who had been crucified in the anatomically correct loci, the wrists; whose blood running down the arms had drips responding to gravity at the correct angles for the position of the arms in a crucifixion; whose legs appeared unbroken; who had an ellipsoid lesion in the side, whence cells and serum had come, and, lying on the cloth, had post-mortem blood dribbling out of the wound and puddling along the small of the back; whose lacerating scourge marks were deep enough to be bloody, with serum albumin oozing at the margins; whose feet had been transfixed with a spike and bled; and on the soles of whose feet there was dirt.

All in all, it is a startling medical documentary of what was described so briefly in the Gospels. Nor was there anything else on the Shroud that would *negate* the actual presence of a scourged, crucified man lying in that linen. But exactly whose body was it? Science has no way of determining the answer. We just do not know.

We told the audience what the image was made of — dehydrative acid oxidation of the linen with the formation of a yellow carbonyl chromophore.

Then, of course, there came the other question that we had been wrestling with for nine months: "How did the images get on the cloth?"

We answered by discussing all the possibilities we had been able to conjure up. And then we explained that we had had to reject all of them, one by one.

"Where," we were asked, "does that leave you?"

"We just do not know!"

And that is the nub of it. No member of the team had worked in a vacuum. When confronted with a problem, he would discuss it with other colleagues at his own or other institutions. Each of the forty STURP members must have consulted at least ten other investigators who were not part of the Shroud team. Thus, at least four hundred scientists had added their input. In addition, all of us had given lectures before meetings of Sigma Xi, the scientific society to which most research scientists belong, at chapter meetings of the American Chemical Society, at universities across the country and their alumni groups, such as MIT's, at meetings of other scientific societies — from physical engineering to the medical sciences. From all of these we had received contributions of knowledge and suggestions. But on the subject of how the body images got on the Shroud, every suggestion had been invalidated by the data.

The Shroud remains, as it has over the centuries, a mystery.

Epilogue

So where does all this huge amount of science leave us? The Shroud of Turin is now the most intensively studied artifact in the history of the world. Somewhere between 100,000 and 150,000 scientific man-hours have been spent on it, with the best analytical tools available. The physical and chemical data fit hand in glove. It is certainly true that if a similar number of data had been found in the funerary linen attributed to Alexander the Great, Genghis Khan, or Socrates, there would be no doubt in anyone's mind that it was, indeed, the shroud of that historical person. But because of the unique position that Jesus holds, such evidence is not enough.

I have discussed with most of the team, during the interviews preceding my writing of this book, how they felt about the Shroud. Three of them, John Jackson, Robert Bucklin, and Barrie Schwortz, believe that it is probably the authentic, burial shroud of Jesus of Nazareth. The rest of us have to say that we do not know. There is no such thing as a scientific test for Jesus, and there probably never will be. Tom D'Muhala feels that the Shroud probably fulfills its purpose for each generation and that the "truth," in terms of hard, scientific evidence, may never be found. Most of us who say we do not know will probably say the same even if a carbon 14 examination dates the Shroud as 2000 years old. The point that must be made, and cannot be emphasized too strongly, is that this scientific adventure was just that. Science. It had nothing to do with faith. Don Lynn puts it well. He says of the Shroud:

> It is anatomically accurate; it matches the Gospels historically; everything is correct with what we know. It is an accurate picture of the passion and death of Christ. It makes it very real that this was a man who was beaten and scourged and crucified. So the story is all there. Whether it is authentic or not is not important. What you have is the Gospel, the story of Christ crucified, set forth in detail before you, to look at, appreciate, and think about. Who made it is unimportant. So the final answer is not really that crucial, except as a challenging exercise.

The images are the result of dehydrative acid oxidation of the linen. The blood is human blood. How the images got on the cloth is a mystery. We would love to have the answer to this mystery, to explain the science of it. If it turns out that some form of molecular transport we have not been able to fathom is the method whereby the images of the scourged, crucified man were transferred to the linen, we shall have solved only another little micropart of the puzzle.

We do know, however, that there are thousands on thousands of pieces of funerary linen going back to millennia before Christ, and another huge number of linens of Coptic Christian burials. On none of these is there any image of any kind. A few have some blood and stains on them, but no image.

The Shroud bears the images of a man who has had incredible, violent damage done to his body, yet whose face is filled with serenity and peace. It is an extracanonical witness to what happened to Jesus Christ, whether the man in the Shroud was Jesus or not. Faith stands alone. It needs no buttressing or support from artifacts. The Shroud is an artifact; an interesting and fascinating artifact.

However, there are some remarkable aspects to this voyage of discovery.

The team itself — its formation, cohesion, diversity, collaboration, as well as its sacrifice of time, talent, and treasure — is unique in scientific annals.

The role of "coincidence" is awesome.

Science undertook its specialty, which is measurement. We were supremely confident that the answers would — indeed, must — be forthcoming. And we failed.

Many team members were ordered or threatened to desist from the project, yet they persevered.

Though it was believed that there would be a confrontation between science and religion, none occurred. Rather, the relationship was harmonious and synergistic.

All of us have been changed by the project. I believe we have grown.

Some years ago, a friend of mine said to me in exasperation, "Heller, why don't you spend less time in Athens and more in Jerusalem?"

I find the Acropolis much less inviting these days.

Scientific Bibliography
of the Members of the
Shroud of Turin Research Group

Accetta, J. S., and J. Stephen Baumgart. "Infrared Reflectance Spectroscopy and Thermographic Investigations of the Shroud of Turin." *Applied Optics,* vol. 19, no. 12, 15 June 1980, pp. 1921–1929.

Avis, C., D. Lynn, J. Lorre, S. Lavoie, J. Clark, E. Armstrong, and J. Addington. "Image Processing of the Shroud of Turin." *Proceedings of the 1982 IEEE Conference on Cybernetics and Society,* pp. 554–558.

Bucklin, Robert, M.D., J.D. "The Shroud of Turin: A Pathologist's Viewpoint." *Legal Medicine Annual,* 1981.

Devan, D., and V. Miller. "Quantitative Photography of the Shroud of Turin." *Proceedings of 1982 IEEE Conference on Cybernetics and Society,* pp. 548–553.

Ercoline, W. R., J. P. Jackson, and R. C. Downs. "Examination of the Turin Shroud for Image Distortions." *Proceedings of 1982 IEEE Conference on Cybernetics and Society,* pp. 576–579.

Gilbert, Roger, Jr., and Marion M. Gilbert. "Ultraviolet-Visible Reflectance and Fluorescence Spectra of the Shroud of Turin." *Applied Optics,* vol. 19, no. 12, 15 June 1980, pp. 1930–1936.

Heller, John H., and Alan D. Adler. "Blood on the Shroud of

Turin." *Applied Optics*, vol. 19, no. 16, 14 August 1980, pp. 2742–2744.

Heller, J. H., and A. D. Adler. "A Chemical Investigation of the Shroud of Turin." *Canadian Forensic Society Scientific Journal*, vol. 14, no. 3, 1981, pp. 81–103.

Jackson, J. P., E. J. Jumper, and W. R. Ercoline. "Three-Dimensional Characteristics of the Shroud Image." *Proceedings of 1982 IEEE Conference on Cybernetics and Society*, pp. 559–575.

Jumper, E., "An Overview of the Testing Performed by the Shroud of Turin Research Project with a Summary of Results." *Proceedings of 1982 IEEE Conference on Cybernetics and Society*, pp. 535–537.

Jumper, E. J., A. D. Adler, J. P. Jackson, S. F. Pellicori, J. H. Heller, and J. R. Druzik. "A Comprehensive Examination of the Various Stains and Images on the Shroud of Turin." Presented at the September 1982 meeting of the American Chemical Society, Kansas City. To be published in *Advances in Archeological Chemistry*, 1983.

Jumper, Eric J., and Robert W. Mottern. "Scientific Investigation of the Shroud of Turin." *Applied Optics*, vol. 19, no. 12, 15 June 1980, pp. 1909–1912.

Miller, V., and D. Lynn. "DeLijkwade Van Turijn." *Natuur en Techniek*, February 1981, pp. 102–125.

Miller, V. D., and S. F. Pellicori. "Ultraviolet Fluorescence Photography of the Shroud of Turin." *Journal of Biological Photography*, vol. 19, no. 3, July 1981, pp. 71–85.

Morris, R. A., L. A. Schwalbe, and R. J. London. "X-Ray Fluorescence Investigation of the Shroud of Turin." *X-Ray Spectrometry*, vol. 9, no. 2, 1980, pp. 42–47.

Mottern, R. W., R. J. London, and R. A. Morris. "Radiographic Examination of the Shroud of Turin — A Preliminary Report." *Materials Evaluation*, vol. 38, no. 12, 1979, pp. 102–125.

Pellicori, S. F. "Spectral Properties of the Shroud of Turin." *Applied Optics*, vol. 19, no. 12, 15 June 1980, pp. 1913–1920.

Pellicori, S. F., and R. A. Chandos. "Portable Unit Permits UV/Vis Study of 'Shroud.'" *Industrial Research & Development*, February 1981, pp. 186–189.

Pellicori, Samuel, and Mark S. Evans. "The Shroud of Turin Through the Microscope." *Archeology*, January–February 1981, pp. 32–43.

Schwalbe, L. A., and R. N. Rogers. "Physics and Chemistry of the Shroud of Turin: A Summary of the 1978 Investigation." *Analytica Chimica Acta*, vol. 135, 1982, pp. 3–49.

Schwortz, B. "Mapping of Research Test Point Areas on the Shroud of Turin." *Proceedings of 1982 IEEE Conference on Cybernetics and Society*, pp. 538–547.